MAGIC NAMES OF FASHION

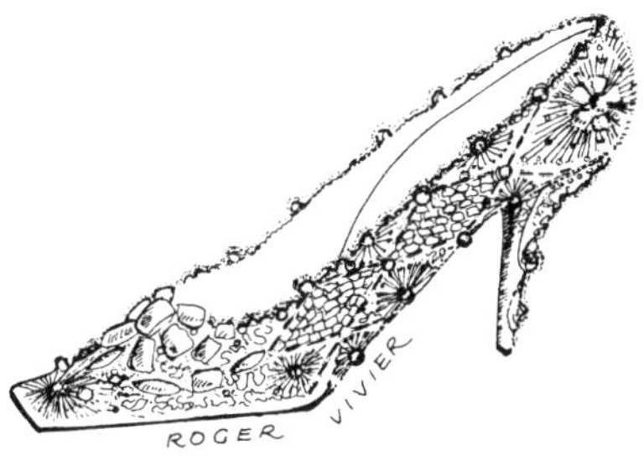

MAGIC NAMES OF FASHION

ERNESTINE CARTER

WEIDENFELD AND NICOLSON
LONDON

First published in Great Britain by
Weidenfeld and Nicolson Ltd
91 Clapham High Street
London SW4 7TA
1980

Designed by Behran Kapadia
Illustrations by Maureen Bourke

ISBN 0 297 77804 8

Filmset by Keyspools Ltd, Golborne, Lancs
Printed in the United States of America

CONTENTS

Author's Acknowledgements 2

Introduction 4

page 6

GEORGE BRYAN 'BEAU' BRUMMELL

1778–1840

page 20

CHARLES FREDERICK WORTH

1825–1895

page 34

MADELEINE VIONNET

1875–1975

page 44

PAUL POIRET

1879–1944

page 52
GABRIELLE 'COCO' CHANEL
1883–1971

page 68
EDWARD MOLYNEUX 1891–1974
MAIN ROUSSEAU BOCHER 'MAINBOCHER' 1890–1976

page 82
ELSA SCHIAPARELLI
1890–1973

page 90
CHRISTIAN DIOR
1905–1957

page 98
CRISTOBAL BALENCIAGA
1895–1972

page 110
EMILIO PUCCI
1914–

page 120
PIERRE CARDIN
1922–

page 128
MARY QUANT 1934–
ANDRE COURREGES 1923–

page 138

Vogue · EDNA WOOLMAN CHASE 1877–1951
CARMEL SNOW 1887–1961 · *Harper's Bazaar*

page 149

W AND JOHN FAIRCHILD
1927–

page 160

DIANA VREELAND
190?–

page 174

LAURA ASHLEY
1926–

page 182

CLAIRE McCARDELL 1905–1958
BONNIE CASHIN 190?–
CALVIN KLEIN 1942–

page 192

YSL (YVES SAINT LAURENT)
1936–

Epilogue 213
Bibliography 214
Index 219

To the Memory of

SIR CECIL BEATON

The Most Magic Name of All

AUTHOR'S ACKNOWLEDGEMENTS

My deepest debt of gratitude is to the late Sir Cecil Beaton whose book *The Glass of Fashion* has been an invaluable reference ever since I first made its acquaintance. It was a source of great pleasure to me that, before his death, Sir Cecil allowed me to show my appreciation by accepting the dedication of this, my latest effort. Sir Cecil was the first to write about the people who make fashion rather than only about fashion itself. His graceful, discursive, and always informative prose serves as a model but, alas, one that it is impossible to emulate. He had the good fortune to know the personalities about whom he wrote, which gave him the opportunity of sketching in words, as well as pencil, vivid portraits. His sharp eye, acting as the lens of his favourite camera, caught every detail, which his very personal perception turned into irresistible quotations.

Second only to Sir Cecil is my debt to Gail Rummell who with the patience of an angel has helped me dig out sources, check dates and quotations, and with cheerful courage has tackled the translation of my rough typescript into tidy pages, a task closely resembling the deciphering of the Rosetta stone. In addition, a dedicated grammarian, she has vetted each sentence mercilessly. Any solecisms are due entirely to my stubbornness in occasionally preferring to have my own way.

I should also like to thank Maureen Bourke for the skill and understanding with which she has interpreted what started out as a light-hearted experiment into witty and accomplished illustrations.

Especially I should like to thank the artists and photographers who provided the inspiration for her drawings.

Finally I am grateful to the following who have helped me beyond the call of duty: John Dreyfus, typographer, for suggesting the typeface Spectrum in which the body of the book is set; Bernard Laser, Managing Director of Condé Nast Publications, and Beatrix Miller, Editor of *Vogue*, for kindly putting the resources of the magazine and its staff at my disposal, with especial thanks to Sheila Wetton, Senior Fashion Editor, for sharing her reminiscences of her years at Molyneux in London; Andrew Naylor, Librarian of the Royal United Services Institution for Defence Studies, for untangling the history of Beau Brummell's regiment; Dr Malcolm Rogers of the National Portrait Gallery for a run-down of the fabrics used in Restoration portraits; the National Film Archive for tracking down dress designers for films; Madeleine Ginsburg of the Victoria & Albert Museum for checking the source of a quote; the Library of the *Sunday Times* for finding the impossible; Anne Boyd of the *Observer* and Hébé Dorsey of the *International Herald Tribune* for so obligingly sending me clippings of their pages I had missed; Renée Taylor for wheedling information from Chanel; Betty Britten for the latest background on Courrèges; Moira Braybrooke of Laura Ashley, and Brig Davis of Mary Quant for their efficient publicity material; Casey Tolar of Fashion Promotions for winkling out facts and figures from *Women's Wear Daily*; Percy Savage of Fashion Promotions and Peter Hope Lumley for current fashion gossip; Sue Railey for undertaking chores in Paris; Bernadine Morris of the *New York Times*; Elizabeth Anne Coleman, Curator of Costumes and Textiles at the Brooklyn Museum, Suzanne Gleaves, Anne Coffin and Helen Carlton for excavations in New York; and last but not least, Christian, Lady Hesketh, for priceless nuggets from her mine of Scottish lore.

INTRODUCTION

It is a truth universally acknowledged that anthologists are inevitably criticized more for what they leave out than for what they include, and as Lord Trevelyan once said, reviewers always seem to write about the book they think one should have written instead of that which has just been painfully completed. In an attempt to dodge the more obvious brickbats I therefore hasten to say at once that I am deeply conscious of certain omissions. In extenuation I plead that magic is not always a question of degree of skill or even success. It is as mysterious as star quality. Some have it; some, equally deserving, don't.

I pondered long and hard over outstanding talents like Madame Grès, Hubert de Givenchy, Marc Bohan at Christian Dior, Fortuny, Valentino, Charles James, Jean Muir, Zandra Rhodes, Bill Gibb, Valentina, Bill Blass, Halston, Oscar de la Renta . . . the list is as long as there are designers of character and originality, but it would take an encyclopaedia to do justice to them all. My final choice may seem arbitrary, even capricious, and I have been on the receiving end of heated arguments in favour not only of the designers mentioned above, but of others as well. I will admit that I have given way over one name which is more than possibly arguable – but I shall leave it to the reader to decide which one that is.

Shakespeare's much quoted apothegm about greatness adapts with strange ease to magic: some are born with it, some achieve it, and some have it thrust upon them. Examples of the first category are Dior and Quant, whose names have the advantage of Gertrude Stein's Josephine in Lord Berner's *Wedding Bouquet* of being the same in every language. Chanel with her abrasive will is the archetype of the second, while the reclusive Balenciaga typifies the third. What criteria I used as yardsticks against which to measure my magic names are hard to define. I should like to brush this off with the well-worn Civil Service answer of 'I'm glad you asked that question', and turn to the next. But of course I can't. First the names had to survive – or have a sporting chance to do so. The last is tricky, for the comets of today may be the meteorites of tomorrow. Second, those who bear or bore these magic names should have changed the course and shape of fashion, should have taken it by the shoulders, given it a smart shake and started it off in a new direction. To do this, such personalities must be so positive, so individual, so incorrigibly original that their imprint is immediately recognizable and indelibly stamped not only on clothing but on the taste and style of living of their time.

Such dominance can be accomplished by precept as well as example. Beau Brummell surveyed his world through an eyeglass: Saint Laurent peers at his through horn-rimmed spectacles. The Beau's monocle was trained only on men's clothing; Saint Laurent's twin lenses encompass wear for both sexes. Both influence, and influenced, by example. Others can influence by precept. Not all who exercise an influence on fashion are designers. There are creative editors like Carmel Snow, astute critics like Eugenia Sheppard, imaginative entrepreneurs like Diana Vreeland, provocative trade publishers like John Fairchild. Each in his or her way has contributed to the myriad facets of that intangible whole: fashion.

BRUMMELL

GEORGE BRYAN 'BEAU' BRUMMELL

1778–1840

Man and Myth

Of all the magic names of Fashion, George Bryan Brummell's is the most potent. That the magic is based on the myth and not the man is unimportant; perhaps the myth has added to its potency. It would be impossible to enumerate all the books which have been written about him or those in which he has appeared, for no history of George IV or his period is complete without him, nor any autobiography by, nor biography about, persons who knew or knew about him. The bibliography stretches from the biography written by Captain William Jesse, which appeared four years after Brummell's melancholy end, to that by Hubert Cole in 1977.

The Beau was also the subject of two books written during his lifetime: *Granby* by T.H. Lister 1825, in which he appeared as 'Trebeck', where he was given the 'nameless grace of polished ease'; and *Pelham* by Bulwer Lytton 1828, who satirized him as 'Russelton'. The latter book, according to Jesse, displeased the Beau, who dismissed it as 'the grossest caricature'. He was portrayed on the New York stage in 1893–4 by the then popular actor Richard Mansfield in Clyde Fitch's successful play eponymously titled *Beau Brummell*. His myth was also set to music by the French composer Reynaldo Hahn in an opera composed in 1931.

His image, or what purports to be his image, extends even farther into the twentieth century and will be perpetuated until the demise of the *New Yorker* magazine. For its first cover on 21 February 1925, the editor, Harold Ross, commissioned artist Rea Irwin to do a drawing of what Brendan Gill calls 'a Beau Brummell-like dandy', a drawing which has appeared ever since on every anniversary issue. It amazed Gill that Ross' advisory board – which included George Kaufman, Dorothy Parker, Alice Duer Miller and Alexander Woollcott as well as Rea Irwin, a worldly, knowledgeable, scathingly sarcastic lot if ever there was one – would approve the choice of what he describes as 'an early nineteenth-century English fop, scrutinizing through a monocle, with a curiosity so mild that it amounts to disdain, a passing butterfly' to symbolize the 'racy and sophisticated new publication'. Ross, it is agreed, was a brilliant editor, though with great open spaces where his education might have been. He might, therefore, be forgiven for having accepted Irwin's visualization of Brummell as the preposterous fop, the exaggerated dandy, but his intuition was correct, for Brummell himself was all that Ross hoped the new magazine would be: sophisticated, witty, and if not 'racy', at least fearless in repartee. Ross perceived the man; Irwin, the myth, although he seems to have done a bit of homework, for the butterfly might possibly be a subtle reference to some verses written by Brummell in 1806, presumably on the death of the lovely, ever-loving and much-loved Georgiana, Duchess of Devonshire, which he entitled 'Butterfly's Funeral'. On the other hand, the butterfly might have been a passing salute to Whistler. Anyway, there is no evidence in actual or word portraits that Brummell ever used an eyeglass, disdainfully or otherwise.

Perhaps the strangest (and the latest) tribute to the lasting reputation of the Beau as the arbiter of elegance came in a 1979 BBC television programme on Groucho Marx in which Groucho's son was interviewed. 'My father', he reminisced with masterly understatement, 'was no Beau Brummell.'

The myth is most beguilingly and elegantly burnished with a touch as light as the brush of a moth's wing by that whimsical exquisite, Sir Max Beerbohm. In the collection of essays he titled with customary modesty *The Works of Max Beerbohm*, published in 1923, he gave Mr Brummell pride of place in his chapter on 'Dandies and Dandies' (first published in 1895 as a magazine piece. Mr Beerbohm as he was then, although he accepted the prevalent estimate of Beau Brummell as a dandy, takes a leaf from Mark Antony's funeral oration for Caesar and deftly turns the essay into a defence of dandyism and with it of Brummell.

The whole piece is such a perfect soufflé that one hesitates to take a spoonful of quotations for fear that the whole delicate structure might fall. It is, however, irresistible. After teasing Brummell and his fellow dandies like a Persian cat playing with a catnip ball, he admits that 'in all known images' of the Beau 'we are struck by the utter simplicity of his attire'. (Byron, too, is said to have found nothing remarkable in his dress 'save a certain exquisite propriety'.) After agreeing with Barbey d'Aurevilly that Brummell was 'the supreme king of the dandies' and one whose life was devoted solely to being a dandy, Beerbohm argues that 'it is as an artist, and for his supremacy in the art of costume as in itself an art, and for that superb taste and subtle simplicity of mode whereby he was able to expel, at length, the Byzantine spirit of exuberance which had possessed St James's and wherefore he is justly called the Father of Modern Costume that I do most deeply revere him.' He affects to believe that it is right that Brummell should have no interest other than the production of the work of art which was himself, an assessment previously agreed by Barbey d'Aurevilly (1884). Then in a lapidary phrase Beerbohm adds, 'Like the single-minded artist that he was, he turned full and square toward his art and looked life straight in the face out of the corners of his eyes.' Surely the last typically Beerbohm paradox implies that Brummell was not as 'single-minded' as Beerbohm has pretended to believe or that he took his 'art' or his life all that seriously.

Although Sir Max would not have known how to mount a soap-box if one were placed at his feet, nor would he ever have allowed himself the impassioned partisan posture which earned Alexander Woollcott the sobriquet of 'a butterfly in heat', he comes near to hyperbole when he declares that:

> The costume of the nineteenth century as shadowed for us first by Mr Brummell, so quiet, so reasonable, and I say emphatically, so beautiful; free from folly or affection, yet susceptible to exquisite ordering; plastic, austere, economical, may not be ignored ... I doubt even if any soever gradual evolution will lead us astray from the general precepts of Mr Brummell's code.

Alas, writing in 1895 (and re-writing in 1923) the adorable Max could not foresee the excesses of attire, almost as Byzantine as those against which Brummell rebelled, that were to overtake us from the mid-Sixties to mid-Seventies, excesses described by Dr Roy Strong in a BBC radio talk as 'unmatched since the days of pre-Revolutionary Europe'.

This is forgivable; few of us have crystal balls. However, in the erection of his delicate structure, Sir Max drops one or two bricks – one of which has become the corner-stone of the myth. The sentence in which it occurs is so perfectly phrased that no one can wonder that it has survived just short of a century since it was first penned: 'In certain congruities of dark cloth, in the rigid perfection of his linen, in the symmetry of his glove in his hand, lay the secret of Mr Brummell's miracles.' The brick is contained in two words of this otherwise matchless description of the Beau's attire. The words are 'dark cloth', and they are guilty of having given rise to the impression that the Beau introduced the wearing of black and white for evening dress. Although an acquaintance, Lord William Pitt-Lennox, is quoted as saying he eschewed colour (as well as 'trinkets and gewgaws' – not for him Count D'Orsay's multitude of rings or Disraeli's tangle of delicate gold chains), the colours he eschewed were the dragonfly effects which so delighted George IV, both when he was Prince of Wales and King. A much-quoted description traced by Christopher Hibbert to the St James's Chronicle of 1791 of the royal dress worn at Windsor on his father's birthday gives a clue. The Chronicle reports the costume in breathless detail:

a bottle-green and claret-coloured striped silk coat and breeches and a silver tissue waistcoat, very richly embroidered in silver and stones and coloured silks in curious devices and bouquets of flowers. The coat and waistcoat embroidered down the seams and spangled all over the body. The coat cuffs the same as the waistcoat. The breeches were likewise covered in spangles. Diamond buttons to the coat, waistcoat and breeches, which with his brilliant diamond epaulettes and sword, made the whole dress form a most magnificent appearance.

By contrast Brummell did seem to 'eschew colour', but Captain Jesse reports that for evening his coat was blue and his silk stockings striped. With a white waistcoat and black 'pantaloons buttoned tight to the ankle', his appearance was in direct contrast to that of the Prince. Later, Jesse writes, Brummell added a velvet collar to his blue coat, changed his waistcoat from white to buff, and slimmed his pantaloons into trousers. Jesse adds what he had failed to mention before – the characteristic white neckcloth. The combination of blue and buff which Brummell had always favoured for day was that of the American Army worn by the Whigs to show sympathy with the rebels. It was somewhat contrary that Brummell should adopt these colours in view of the fact that it is his father's patron, Lord North, who is commonly given the credit for losing England the colonies.

As for the congruities of dark cloth and white linen, Jesse tells of an evening when he was, as he puts it, *'costumé'* thus, at which the Beau remarked: 'My dear Jesse, I am sadly afraid that you have been reading *Pelham*, but excuse me, you look very much like a magpie.' It seems possible that Beerbohm omitted to read Jesse.

The myths are myriad, some plainly encouraged by Brummell himself: stories that he had his gloves made by two glove-makers, one for the thumbs and the other for the fingers and hand; that he required three barbers to do his hair to his satisfaction and that he had his boots polished with champagne. The story which one would think he enjoyed is the one quoted by Tenenbaum that he would bathe for two hours, for cleanliness at a time when scent was substituted for soap was one of his revolutionary and real obsessions. He wished to make cleanliness, if not next to godliness, an essential element of fashion.

This was the man behind the myth; and the man, fastidious both morally and physically, good-looking, with a gift for repartee, liked by men and adored by women, is far more interesting than the myth. In his distaste for the drunkards and gamblers, the roués and spendthrifts that made up the society of the time, he may have decided to do what Disraeli was to do when, realizing that few people liked to read serious pamphlets, he embedded his political views in successful baroque novels. Similarly, Brummell may have chosen to conceal his serious concern under a veneer of exaggerated frivolity. That, fundamentally, he was serious is given as one of the reasons that the Duchess of York welcomed him into the select coterie that formed around herself and the Duke, and remained a loyal friend until her death. In her view, according to Melville, 'the Beau had lifted the morals and deportment of English society'. Should this hypothesis be valid, and he did feel that if people were clean in their person, they would be less apt to be squalid in their habits, he anticipated the Behaviourists of nearly a century later. If this was his end, his aptitude for elegance and his sense of timing were priceless tools.

He began his career, not as a Beau but as a Buck, at Eton, where he was sent when he was twelve (according to Jesse and the eleventh edition of the *Encyclopaedia Britannica*; Cole says eight) by his father, who had been Private Secretary to Lord North throughout the latter's tenure as Prime Minister, and who afterwards became High Sheriff of Berkshire. (There are various accounts about *his* father – that he was in trade or in service – but all agree that he was of low degree.) At Eton, Brummell was no scruffy schoolboy. Even at that untender age, he added a fillip to the school uniform, as Connely observed, 'wearing the wings of his cravat not only longer than it was customary but more neatly tied, overlapping the lapels of his coat.' It is also said that he added a gold buckle to his white stock. Even when the Buck went to play football a contemporary remembers that his striped worsted stockings were 'quite clean and tight'. He was also popular, and as several biographers note, he had acquired 'that worldly air that Eton peculiarly bestows'.

It was while he was at Eton that he was presented to the Prince of Wales, later Prince Regent and eventually, at the age of fifty-seven, King George IV. The Prince was apparently much struck by the precocious aplomb of this witty, well-dressed, diverting youth, and the meeting was destined to ripen into intimacy.

Brummell next went on to Oriel College, Oxford, where he added to his reputation for elegance in appearance and manners, that of wit and raconteur, and, in coming second for the Newdigate Prize for Poetry, showed no mean literary ability. (Much later, in 1822, he wrote a book, *A History of Male and Female Costume from Ancient Greece to Modern Times*, which was not published until 1932. Despite its portentous title, it does not appear to have been a success.)

His Oxford career was brief, limited to the Trinity term. He left in 1794 at the age of sixteen, and that year he took up, on 10 June, the cornetcy which the Prince of Wales had offered to him in the 10th (Prince of Wales's) Regiment of Light Dragoons. The cornetcy was not a great commission but with it went the privilege of carrying the colours. That same year, on 10 October, Brummell was made lieutenant, and two years later on 1 June he was gazetted captain. It has been hinted that he spent more time with his royal patron than with his men, so much so that it was said that he did not know his own troops, even when on parade.

There are several theories why he sold his commission, which he did the next year on 7 September 1797. Jesse suggests that he may have been tired of powdering his hair, a custom that was going out of fashion anyway. Cole offers the hypothesis that it was because he had succeeded to an inheritance variously estimated from £20,000 to £50,000 – in those days a fortune. Beerbohm characteristically spins a cobweb of a tale. His version is that Brummell could not bear to wear the same uniform as the other officers and turned up for parade in 'a pale blue tunic with silver epaulettes'. When his colonel remonstrated, Brummell saluted and left, not only the parade-ground but the army as well. Another version still lives in the regiment. The Prince of Wales, unable to resist the temptation to dress in the latest style and somewhat jealous that every European country had formed Hussar regiments in imitation of the Hungarians, obtained sanction in 1806 from his father to 'recognize and equip' his regiment as the 10th Royal Hussars, as they are known today. It was the first regiment in the British Army to be so designated. The Dragoons had been conveniently quartered at Brighton; the contemporary version goes that when Brummell was informed that they would be moving north to the provincial city of Manchester, he said he had not reckoned on foreign service when he joined up. Both Jesse and Cole turn this tale into a rather discreditable story of obsequious flattery to the Prince.

In any case Brummell retired from the army. With his new fortune he set up a bachelor establishment in London and took his place in the society with which he was already familiar. Known to be an intimate of the Prince and with his own attractions, all doors were open to him. Dukes, duchesses, lords and ladies, knights – the cream of the peerage were his friends, and he was at home in their castles and stately homes where he was soon accepted as the *arbiter elegantiarum*.

Brummell had for some time been gently influencing the Prince towards the painstaking grooming, the meticulous cleanliness, the fine polish, as well as the gentle art of handling a snuff-box, which were his own hallmarks. This must have been an uphill job, for the Prince was, to put it mildly, a dressy man. Another of his ensembles, which nearly rivals the one previously described, is recalled by a contemporary, Cyrus Redding, and quoted by Beerbohm: 'deep brown velvet, silver-embroidered, with cut-steel buttons, and a gold net thrown over all.' The beautiful idiocy of the gold net renders the reader speechless.

It may be true that the Prince was persuaded into the neckcloths, which were Brummell's outward and visible sign of an inward and spiritual grace, by a desire to conceal an attack of swollen glands.

This is a bit too much like the story that Worth invented the crinoline to disguise Empress Eugénie's pregnancy to be taken without a grain of salt. However, he did accept it and in a 'quadruple stock of great dimension' it looked to a young observer, according to Christopher Hibbert, as if the Royal chin was always struggling to emerge.

This effect could not have pleased Brummell, who paid as much attention to the proportion of his neckcloths as to their spotlessness. Creased linen was anathema to him, and to keep his in the 'rigid perfection' Beerbohm describes, he introduced the use of starch. Alan Palmer in 1972 quotes *The English Spy* of 1826: 'When he first appeared in this stiffened cravat, its sensation was prodigious; dandies were struck dumb with envy, and washerwomen miscarried.'

The actual tying of the neckcloth was a ritual which gave rise to the story that a mid-morning caller found Brummell standing in a sea of crumpled neckcloths. In answer to the visitor's query, the valet explained, 'These, Sir, are our failures.' The neckcloths became not only a fashion but a fad, and in 1806 inspired a pamphlet, half-serious, half-spoof, called 'Neckclothitania or Tietania: Being an Essay on Starches'. Twelve years after Brummell's departure for France, the neckcloths were still going strong enough for a book to be published giving step-by-step instructions for tying thirty-two variations.

Every description of Brummell contradicts the legend that he was a fop. Moderation, good taste, propriety, lack of eccentricity or extravagance are words which occur over and over again. Brummell himself, quoted by Melville, gives the best description of his principles of dress: 'the severest mortification a gentleman could incur would be to attract observation in the street by his outward appearance'. It was scarcely his fault that society up to the Throne itself copied his clothes, his mannerisms, his choice of knick-knacks, especially his snuff-boxes and the nonchalant grace with which he used them. As for his being a Dandy, it was Byron who nicknamed Wattier's eating-club the Dandy's Club. As a matter of fact, Brummell also belonged to Brooks's and White's, as did the Prince and their special set.

That he was witty is conceded, but wit dates. One story, however, has such a contemporary flavour that it seems worth repeating. A valet whom he was interviewing asked for a wage of £150 a year, to which Brummell replied, 'Make it £200 and *I'll* work for *you*.' It was this quick tongue that was to prove his undoing.

The Prince, by now the Regent, became rather resentful that Brummell, sixteen years his junior, should be the universally acknowledged arbiter rather than his royal self. Intimacy with royalty is fraught with pitfalls, and one or two incidents led up to the now immortal scene – whether it was on Bond Street, on the Mall, or at a ball at the Argyle Rooms, whether Brummell was with Lord Alvanley or Sir Henry Mildmay does not matter. The Prince spoke to his companion but cut Brummell, whereupon the Beau asked, loudly enough for the Prince to hear, 'Tell me, Alvanley, who is your fat friend?' These eight fatal words marked the end of their friendship – and the end of Brummell, too. In 1816 he fled to France, where he eventually died in exile and penury, his exile lasting twice as long as his brief reign.

The Beau's actual innovations in fashion were far-reaching rather than world-shaking. He introduced the use of starch for the sake of tidiness. Disliking wrinkled trousers he developed various ways of keeping his straight – by buttons and then by straps beneath the arch of the foot, anticipating ski pants. He cuffed his riding boots with white leather instead of brown for no apparent reason, except perhaps that they looked smarter. His real innovations were far more important: the habit of cleanliness, neatness and courtesy, of style without ostentation, moderation in eating and drinking without priggishness.

His rise in society may have been in part due to the patronage of the Prince, but he stayed there on his own merits. In an effete age he was not effeminate. As a contemporary, Tom Raikes, wrote in his journals:

> Everyone from the highest to the lowest conspired to spoil him, and who that knew him well could deny that with all his faults he was still the most gentlemanlike, the most agreeable of companions? Never was there a man who during his career had such unbounded influence, and, what is seldom the case, such general popularity in Society. ... He was the idol of the women. Happy was she in whose opera-box he would pass an hour, at whose table he would dine, or whose assembly he would honour. And why? Not only because he was a host of amusement in himself ... but because he was such a favourite with the men that all were anxious to join the party.

It was not because of his snowy neckcloths and taut trousers that Lady Hester Stanhope, when in dire straits in Lebanon and visited in 1830 by Captain Yorke, asked only for news of the Duke of Wellington and George Brummell. '... these two', Captain Yorke reported, 'being the only persons of her country for whom she seemed to entertain any interest.' Nor was it his attire alone that prompted Lord Byron to remark that 'There are only three great men in the nineteenth century, Brummell, Napoleon and myself' – all three of whom, he was to add ruefully, came to grief in the same year.

It is melancholy to think that this man who, by his insistence on perfection of cut and fit, raised the level of British tailoring to a commanding position in the world, whose example influenced the customs of a society, should be popularly remembered as a preposterous fop or as the audacious commoner whose irrepressible tongue led him, when cut by his erstwhile royal patron, to dare to call a fat Prince fat to his face.

C F
WORTH

CHARLES FREDERICK WORTH

1825–1895

Monarch of the Belle Epoque

For over thirty years Worth, according to the *Encyclopaedia Britannica* (the 11th edition) 'set the taste and ordained the fashion of Paris'; in an unusually expansive mood the *Encyclopaedia* adds 'and extended his sway over all the civilized and much of the uncivilized world'. How much this sway depended on the crinoline, the *Encyclopaedia* does not vouchsafe. Worth's ascendancy over the 'civilized' world of the time is uncontested; by the 'uncivilized', the *Encyclopaedia* may have been referring to the years after 1854 when the vast expansion of the railways brought an influx of foreigners to Paris from the United States of America, as well as Russia, Turkey, Egypt, China and points east. The French sneered at these visitors as 'barbarians', even while waxing rich at their expense.

Worth's early days are too well known to repeat in detail. He was born in the small provincial town of Bourne in Lincolnshire, where his father was a country solicitor with a fatal weakness for gambling. Because of his father's profligacy, the boy found himself in London, at the age of twelve, as an apprentice in the still enduring though now less grand store of Swan & Edgar. At that time, in its present superb position at the point where Piccadilly and Regent Street converge into Piccadilly circus at the southern end of John Nash's noble quadrant, it was famous and fashionable. In 1837 it gave Worth a vantage point from which to observe the smart world. He concluded, apparently, that this world derived its smartness from Paris fashions, for at twenty, with no capital, no friends or introductions and not a word of French, he set off for that city – a trip which, although undoubtedly begun in trepidation, was to end in triumph.

From his first job in a modest draper's, he somehow found his way to one of the most fashionable shops in Paris – Gagelin et Opigez, famous for their fine silks and cashmere shawls with a minor line in ready-made cloaks and coats. Worth found the fabrics beautiful but the clothes conventional and monotonously the same. This was because people were still nervous of adventurous spending after the horrors of the desperate street-fighting of 1848. Another and different result of the riots was the creation of the Paris of today. The Emperor lost no time in giving Baron Haussman a free hand (no nonsense about preservation of historic buildings or monuments) in planning well-lighted boulevards on which, it was hoped, barricades could not be easily erected.

The Revolution of 1848 was only the beginning of twenty-three years which were so action-packed that, to paraphrase Saki, France unfortunately made more history than it could consume. Worth lived and worked through it all. His professional life encompassed the deposition and flight of the King, Louis Philippe, after the Revolution of 1848; the establishment of the Second Republic with Louis Napoleon, Napoleon's nephew, as President; the coup of 1851 which made Louis Napoleon Emperor, marking the death of the Second Republic and the birth of the Second Empire over which Eugénie, whom the Emperor had married in 1853, reigned, not only as Empress of France, but as Queen of Fashion. This began the happiest period of Worth's professional life.

Then came the Crimean War of 1854–5; the execution in 1867 of the Archduke Maximilian, whom Napoleon III had made Emperor of Mexico, and whose death plunged the Court into mourning; the Franco-Prussian War of 1870 and the Revolution which followed the surrender at Sedan, not only of half the army but also of the Emperor himself, who was taken prisoner. This disaster which opened the door for the Third Republic, born of the fury of the populace, forced the Empress to flee to England and brought the Second Empire and Worth's halcyon years to an end.

There followed the bitter siege of Paris until, in 1871, starvation brought about its capitulation and the brief occupation by the Germans which culminated in the Commune and civil war and the election of Thiers as President of the Third Republic. All of this Worth, like the Abbé Sièyes, survived. Like another more eminent

Frenchman, Talleyrand, he adjusted himself to the changing winds of fortune.

Presidents' wives, as well as empresses, needed clothes. So did the ladies of the *demi-monde* and the stars of the stage. In an interview he gave to a British magazine in 1871, Worth showed himself uninterested in theories about the relation of fashion to wars, conveniently forgetting 'Sebastapol blue' and 'Crimean green'. He did, however, reveal that the Russians and the Americans were his best clients.

Of the Americans, Edith Wharton in *The Age of Innocence*, writing about New York in the 1870s, poked gentle fun at their prudish attitude to fashion. It was, she wrote, considered 'vulgar to dress in the newest fashions'. Ladies, following the dictum of Boston (then more aristocratic than New York), after ordering their annual wardrobes from Worth, laid them down like port to 'let them mellow' for two years, and even then sometimes dared to alter them. About the mellowers one of her characters remarks about another:

> Old Mrs Baxter Pennilow, who did everything handsomely, used to import twelve a year, two velvet, two satin, two silk, and the other six of poplin and the finest cashmere. It was a standing-order, and as she was ill for two years before she died they found forty-eight Worth dresses that had never been taken out of their tissue paper; and when the girls left off their mourning they were able to wear the first lot at the Symphony concerts without looking in advance of fashion.

Of the alterers, another character remarks, 'The extravagance ... Jane Merry's dress was the only one I recognized from last year; and even that had had the front panel changed. Yet I know she got it out from Worth only two years ago, because my seamstress always goes to make over her Paris dresses before she wears them.' It is not known if Worth was aware of this timidity and, even worse, the tampering with his creations, but it might have comforted him to know that in the New York and Boston of that period a Paris dress was synonymous with Worth.

In that same interview, Worth dismissed Englishwomen as parsimonious. Nearly ten years later Lillie Langtry was happily to prove him wrong. After being introduced to the glories of Worth in 1880 by the Prince of Wales, who, according to Noël B. Gerson in *Lillie Langtry*, bought her an entire wardrobe there, she never looked back. The Jersey Lily bought by the trunkload – in 1883 her purchases filled twenty-two large steamer trunks; in 1891, after she had begun her stage career, she purchased seventeen trunks of new dresses. The next year a jealous lover, maddened by drink, as well as beating her up, tore her new dresses to shreds. Then, penitent, he gave her, along with gifts of fabulous jewels and useful things like race-horses, fifty dresses from Worth. Her stage career seemed founded on her Worth wardrobes, the critics praising them when they could not praise her. None of the clients, however, profligate as they may seem, could touch the Empress, who in 1868 for the opening of the Suez Canal felt she could do for this one occasion with no less than 250 Worth dresses.

While still at Gagelin, Worth was bursting with ideas, and the firm evidently gave him his head. He wanted to design and make to order beautiful clothes from the sumptuous fabrics at hand. He also wanted to marry a beautiful apprentice at the shop. In both desires he was successful, and both were to change his life. For both of them, however, he had to wait; for the latter it was a question of money; for the former, the firm demurred at first, then gave way, acquiring the kudos of launching a major talent and the transformation of dressmaking into *haute couture* – and incidentally making a great deal of money in the process.

Although there is general agreement about these early days of Worth's progress, from here on chroniclers differ, depending, it seems, on how much the writers admired the man. It is a fact that at the Great Exhibition of 1851 in London, the Maison Gagelin won the only Gold Medal awarded to France, but not all agree that Worth must have had a hand in designing the shawls and dresses which were exhibited. They cannot, however, argue that in the Exhibition of 1855, which took place in Paris, his white silk, gold-embroidered court train won the Award.

It is also disputed whether or not he was the inventor of the crinoline on which his fame was built, and with which his name is still associated. It does not matter if he invented it himself or knew how best to utilize an invention brought to him. Like every innovation, the credit is given to the person who popularizes and markets it successfully. This Worth certainly did. There is also some divergence of opinion whether Worth introduced the crinoline before or after he left Gagelin. Several dates are given for the crinoline as Worth used it – made of horsehair and whale-bones, for there had of course been earlier versions. One date is 1856, but 1855 is more generally accepted, although the *Shorter Oxford English Dictionary* puts what they call a 'hoop-petticoat', which was made similarly, as early as 1851. In her caption to an illustration from *Le Petit Courier des Dames* of 1856, reproduced in *Fashion and Fashion Plates*, Doris Langley Moore refers to it as 'just patented'. In the Exhibition of 1855 one of the eye-catchers had been Winterhalter's now famous portrait of the Empress Eugénie with her ladies. The Empress's dress, as described by Norman Hartnell in *Royal Courts of Fashion*, was of 'filmy white gauze over white silk, with blue ribbons to match her eyes'. As it is agreed that Worth did not meet the Empress until 1860, this dress, it is supposed, may have been ordered for her from Gagelin by one of her ladies. All are wearing crinolines, and all have bodices cut to show off to advantage their smooth, sloping white shoulders. The dresses bear a family resemblance to each other and to those being made by Worth at Gagelin.

Anyway, the invention of the crinoline itself was inevitable. Skirts had been getting fuller and fuller since 1836, held out by multitudinous petticoats, then cone-shaped contraptions of steel wire, later even steel watch-spring. Someone was bound to invent a framework that gave the desired effect without the weight of petticoats or complications of wires or springs. Worth's crinoline became the uniform of the Second Empire.

The evidence seems to prove that Worth was making his crinolines before he left Gagelin, which he did in 1858, after twelve years. With a young Swede, Otto Bobergh, Worth set up in the Rue de la Paix, which one admiring chronicler says he 'invented' (presumably in the same way as Poiret 'invented' the Elysées, and Balenciaga the Avenue George V). The going was not too good at first, but the tide was turned for him by the Princess Metternich, wife of the new Austrian Ambassador, of whom he and his wife had caught a glimpse as she drove in her carriage to the Palace of the Tuileries. Both Worths were taken with her aristocratic bearing, and the shy Madame Worth made a startling resolve: to take one of her husband's sketchbooks to show to the Princess. The Princess was as enchanted with the sketches as with Worth's acceptance of the rather meagre sum of 300 francs each, a price she stipulated for the two dresses she ordered. It was well worth (no pun intended) slashing prices to acquire so distinguished a patroness. The Princess also promised to wear one of these dresses at the next ball at the Tuileries.

In what James Pope-Hennesy called 'that delicious atmosphere of sumptuous second-rate', women's dresses were almost overwhelmingly ornate. Worth, following Brummell's example, plumped for restraint, and made for the Princess a dress of white tulle and silver lamé, trimmed only with marguerites. According to another authority, the white tulle was silver-threaded, and the garnish 'bunches of pink cowslips half-hidden in tufts of grass', to which the Princess added 'a wealth of diamonds'. Both agree that it was sashed in white satin. Whether it was the fresh simplicity of the one or the whimsical invention of the other, the dress caught the eye of the Empress, who asked the Princess to arrange for Worth to come to her at the Tuileries. This famous meeting took place in 1860.

With the Empress as his most dazzling client, all Paris was at his feet and the crowned heads of Europe hastened to follow suit and become his customers. Worth's fortune was made. In the Exhibition of 1867, among the exhibits was one featuring the Paris Couture which proved Colbert, Louis XIV's most important minister, to have been right when he said that: 'Fashion is to France what the gold mines of Peru are to the Spaniard.' Worth was, of course, a star turn, and it enraged the French press, already furious because he was English, that so important a dressmaker should also be a man. Nevertheless the world flocked to his salons, which by 1860 he had become the first to realize should reproduce the ample space, the wide doors and the luxurious decoration of the surroundings in which his clients could and would wear his crinolines. This shows that he was a practical as well as an imaginative man who understood the realities of fashion, as does the fact that five years earlier, after the success of the Exhibition of 1855, he had pioneered the provision of special showrooms for foreign buyers.

Perhaps it was the ease with which Madame Worth sold his clothes off her back that inspired him also to be the first to use living models, a claim subsequently made by Lucile and Poiret.

Print gets so hot it nearly scorches the pages in discussing the theory that Worth was the father of the French couture. He certainly raised dressmaking to a new level, gave it a new dimension. If the higher honour is denied him, it must have been some satisfaction to him when in 1885 his son, Gaston, became President for three years of the women's tailoring, ready-to-wear and couture unions which he later organized into the Chambre Syndicale de la Couture Française. It can also be hoped that Charles Frederick might have been pleased by the appointment of his grandson, Jacques, twice (in 1927–31 and again in 1933–5) as President of the fully-fledged Chambre Syndicale de la Couture Parisienne into which the earlier organization had evolved in 1911.

The success of the crinoline became an albatross to Charles Frederick. He was the victim of the Winterhalter syndrome. Although he proffered a varied menu of rich delights, women continued to prefer the known bread and butter of the crinoline. After all, as the Mad Hatter said, it was the best butter. With the increasing spread of its popularity, it spread in width, became exaggerated, often to absurdity, and many cartoons and jokes were made at its expense. These did not deter its wearers. The crinoline suited the frivolous mood of Paris; it swayed deliciously to the seductive strains of Waldteufel, Offenbach and Johann Strauss the Younger. Strauss had been introduced to Paris by Princess Methernich at one of the countless balls given at the time. Worth, too, was having a ball, dressing all the grand waltzing ladies. As early, however, as 1865, Worth had been designing in a less flamboyant style – narrow skirts with trains, princess dresses where for the first time bodices and skirts were cut in one piece; dresses flat in front with the fullness pulled back into a polonaise, sheathing the figure.

The execution of Maximilian in 1867 and Court mourning put a damper on extravagance and frivolity. The next year Worth simplified his line further, and the Empress, perhaps preferring the straight and narrow after too many years of swinging, bell-like charm, took to it at once. It was at last the end of the crinoline.

Worth not only lived through dramatic events of history but also even more far-reaching technological advances. Two of the most pertinent to him were the widespread use of the sewing-machine from 1851, and the introduction in 1860 of paper patterns, a joint English enterprise of Samuel Beeton and his wife (whose fame as the author of *Household Management* still persists), and Christopher Weldon of Weldon's Patterns. Worth took full advantage of both of these developments to extend the boundaries of his business to what could be considered modern dimensions.

Worth became so established in his field that, as in the next century all witticisms were attributed to Dorothy Parker, all inventions (including the rebirth of the bustle) were attributed to him. This is not unreasonable but it is possible that, as with the crinoline, he promoted it. As has been said of ancient aristocratic families, the originator of the bustle, if not its origins, is lost in the mists of time. The *Shorter Oxford Dictionary* gives 1788 as the date of the first use of the word in fashion: 'a pad or wire framework worn beneath the skirt to expand it behind.' Norman Hartnell, however, dates its first appearance as the early 1860s, when presumably it was simply a way of sweeping the enormous fullness of skirts up and to the back. Like the mechanical foundations of the crinoline, the artificial bustle was evolved to take the load of the fabric, while preserving and ultimately exaggerating its back projection.

These aids were many and ingenious. The 'Canfield' of 1887, according to Pegaret Anthony in *High Victorian* the last to be advertised, could be made to collapse by means of a spring; still another played 'God Save the Queen' rather unpatriotically when the wearer sat down, rather than when she rose. How this steatopygous but curiously charming fashion acquired its connotation with a verb which goes back to 1560 meaning 'to be fussily or noisily active', history does not relate. The wit who originated this remains, like the man who ate the first oyster, an unsung hero and an immortal, for versions of the bustle reappear through the centuries as reminiscences of romantic pastiche, from the classic Vionnet in 1934 to Oscar de la Renta in 1979, YSL in 1980.

That Worth was not a dictator is proven by the refusal of women to drop the crinoline until they were ready to, but in spite of that defeat, his name was so magic, his arts so persuasive, that women were soon delighted to follow his lead, and later that of his son, Jean Philippe, at any cost. As the Duchess in *The Edwardians* says to her housekeeper,

> What odd things one remembers. . . . Would you believe it, Wacey, once

I had a pair of sleeves of rainbow velvet with a white tight-fitting frock by Worth, and a man seeing me struggle to go through a narrow doorway, said, 'Oh, duchess, surely you ought to wear one sleeve at a time.' And after that the sleeves became so tight one could not put on one's little bonnet without undoing one's bodice. . . .

That little bonnet was also due to Worth, who in 1855 had rescued women's faces from the demure shadows of the poke bonnet.

Towards the end of his life, Worth began to retire gradually from the business, which continued to flourish under the direction of his two sons, Gaston the businessman and Jean Philippe the designer, who had entered the firm in 1874, four years after Otto Bobergh had retired with his fortune made. Charles Frederick could look back on his career with satisfaction. He was an Englishman who had conquered Paris and, for a remarkably long time, the world of fashion. He had supported the French textile industry, especially the silk weavers of Lyons whom he persuaded the Empress to patronise. He had dressed the royalty of many worlds – the real royalty, the royalty of the *demi-monde* and that of the stage. As he had exposed women's faces, he had shocked the world by exposing their ankles in his shorter crinolines, more sensible for walking, of 1860. However much the pundits may disagree, he is popularly considered to be the Father of French couture. When he died in 1895 at the age of seventy, he was wealthy and he was famous. In what Norman Hartnell describes as his 'sumptuous Gothic villa' outside Paris, he was happily surrounded by the nostalgic souvenirs which he had rescued from the ransacked Tuileries. Above all, he had created a dynasty to carry on the name of Worth and its label – the use of which he was the first to introduce. (Five years after their father's death, the sons opened an English branch of Worth in an imposing house in Grosvenor Street. The business was sold in 1936; the House, however, although subsequently re-sold, continued to bear the name of Worth until 1976 when the lease expired. The Couture House of Worth in Paris closed in 1956. Both in Paris and

London the name continues though in smaller premises and on a smaller scale.)

As Charles Frederick had turned his back on England, including English fabrics, he might not have minded that in Paris his name was pronounced 'Vort'. Even his photograph is totally unEnglish. The beret cocked to one side, the drooping moustaches, the wrinkled sleeve of his coat make him look as one imagines Inspector Maigret would look: there is the same conscious effect of provincial naivety belied by the shrewd, narrowed eyes. Other Englishmen were to make their debuts in Paris during Worth's reign – Redfern (whose real name was Charles Poynter) in 1842, and Henry Creed in 1855, both specialists in tailoring, but neither could challenge Worth's supremacy. In himself he combined the aptitudes of his sons – the designing talent of Jean Philippe and the business sense of Gaston. These, plus the invaluable asset of timing, proved a redoubtable combination.

VIONNET

MADELEINE VIONNET

1875–1975

Goddess of Cut

Madeleine Vionnet is a magic name to magic names. She is a dressmaker's dressmaker. 'No one', Dior asserted (quoted by Sir Cecil Beaton) 'has ever carried the art of dressmaking further than Vionnet.' Bernard Nevill, the British designer of fabrics, who got to know her well in her late years, says that Balenciaga, who was a friend as well as an admirer, visited her constantly until his retirement. When she became bedridden he made for her a pink printed, silk quilted trouser-suit in which she received visitors, reclining on a chaise longue on pink cushions in her drawing-room/bedroom with its parchment-covered walls. Jacques Worth is said to have considered her the finest technician in the whole fashion world. Molyneux, nostalgically recalling the Twenties, described seeing Madame Martinez de Hoz, the rich and much-admired Brazilian beauty, wearing a white chiffon evening dress by Vionnet, 'the skirt a drift of handkerchief points, cut on that famous Vionnet bias'. Madame de Hoz was one of Vionnet's favourite clients; the top favourite was the tall, darkly-beautiful Italian-born Duchesse de Gramont, of whom Vionnet said, 'If I was making a dress, I had only to ask her to come and try it on, and I knew exactly where it was wrong.'

The designer most influenced by Vionnet's bias cut today is Halston, who in his caftans found the same difficulty – a difficulty Vionnet seemed curiously unaware of or ignored in handling the meeting-point at the low vee neck which divided a bias-cut top or joined two bias-cut sides. In 1926, the Duchesse de Gramont, photographed for *Vogue* by Edward Steichen, placed a magnificent jewel at this strategic point. In 1930 Molyneux characteristically solved the problem with a fabric rose. Halston simply leaves his, just as Vionnet did in the otherwise flawless 'handkerchief' dress (dated 1919–20) shown in 'Inventive Clothes 1909–1939', the first exhibition organized by Diana Vreeland for the Costume Institute of the Metropolitan Museum of Art, New York. The fastening can be best studied in the book of photographs by Irving Penn which evolved from that exhibition. At the exhibition itself, according to Bernard Nevill, 'the Vionnets blew our minds'.

Vionnet was – and is – the idol of fashion journalists. Edna Woolman Chase, editor of all the *Vogues*, wrote that 'Vionnet . . . in my opinion was unique, perhaps the only true creator in our time in the art of *couture*.' Madge Garland describes her simply as 'one of the most original designers ever known . . .' Sir Cecil Beaton wrote, 'Vionnet was a genius in the way she used her materials. With her scissors she changed fashion . . .' In Diana Vreeland's opinion, Vionnet's 'creations were a total work of art . . . . She was without doubt the most admired and important dressmaker of the twentieth century.' It is clear that Vionnet is more than magic. She is a legend.

This is the more extraordinary, for although she lived to be nearly one hundred years old, she did not open her famous house until 1922, closed it in 1940 after the outbreak of the second war, and did not unveil her bias cut until 1926 when she was with Doucet. This cut was her great and lasting contribution to fashion. What was dazzling was not only the cut but her skilful exploitation of all its permutations. It could be used for whole dresses, for dresses with lozenge-shaped or triangular bias insets (sometimes outlined by faggoting), for skirts of tiered bias-cut petals or ending in handkerchief points, or for long panels dropping below the hems. The range of the cut seems endless. It produced godets and flared skirts (although crêpe was a pet fabric, Vionnet even cut heavy tweeds and velvet on the bias). It produced halter necks, cowl necks and, perhaps most technically exciting, dresses that fit without fastenings so that they seemed to float over the body, suggesting without revealing. To achieve her effect, she persuaded fabric manufacturers to weave in greater widths. The Vionnet cut dominated fashion. It has been thought (except by Vionnet herself) to be uncopiable but, alas, this did not prove to be so. It was copied, but never with the virtuosity of its originator.

She was the mistress of cut and drapery, which she worked out on wooden figurines about three feet high, with articulated joints rather like those used in nineteenth-century life classes. Thus she conceived her ideas in the round – the only logical way to clothe the human form. Like Chanel, she had no use for sketches which are inevitably flat. As she told Celia Bértin, 'If I had worked from sketches, I should have influenced fashion in quite a different way.' To her, the only way to discover the potential of a fabric was to work directly with it on what she called 'a lay figure'.

Diana Vreeland quotes Vionnet as saying '. . . I never saw fashion. I don't know what fashion is. I made the clothes I believe in.' The last is indubitably true, but a study of her progress from photographs suggests that, like Mainbocher at a later date, she sniffed the air. In 1925 she showed a scoop-necked shift of the current length, dropping her handkerchief points at either side to just above the ankles. In 1926 when the waistline had settled on the hips and skirts has risen, she designed a blouson top tied to a bow round that widest portion of the female anatomy. In a dress of 1925–6 (some books are more hazy than others on dates) 'the interest', as they used to say at dress shows, was at the back where a soft surplice top (one of her signatures) is knotted and tied at a most awkward point for sitting. In 1927, still in the mood of the moment, she produced a brief pailletted shift, breaking the line only at the left side with a mock belt caught with a buckle, its long ends falling to mid-calf. That year she also showed suits with long blouses or jackets exactly in tune with those of her fellows.

In 1931, when waists were rising and skirts falling, she introduced a long bias skirt flaring from a built-up matador waist, topped with a cowl-necked blouse of filmy chiffon. The next year she repeated this high line, substituting wide culottes for the skirt. These were innovative interpretations, but still they echoed the prevailing trend.

Mrs Vreeland's quotation seems at odds with the observations of

Celia Bértin, who wrote in 1954 from direct experience and a meeting with Vionnet, that Vionnet at the age of seventy-nine 'not only attends all the dress shows and lectures, but regularly dines with such and such *première vendeuse*, buyer, or cloth merchant'. This is supported by Bettina Ballard, who recalled seeing her after the Second World War 'at Pierre Balmain's or Jacques Griffe's openings ... protégés both, whose progress she watches with a school-teacher's interest'. 'Couture', Bertin concludes, 'always occupied her.' More recently, Bernard Nevill confirms this but adds that she always referred to herself simply as 'a dressmaker', the literal but less flossy translation of *couturière*.

Another example of Vionnet's interest in current fashion is provided by Madeleine Ginsburg. Vionnet discovered that her collection of 1934 was out of step with the romantic mood which Robert Piguet had been the first to perceive in the Victorian costumes designed by Molyneux in 1933 for *The Barretts of Wimpole Street*. According to Mrs Ginsburg, Vionnet 'within two weeks of her opening scrapped her entire collection.' Nevertheless, as Mrs Ginsburg quotes from a *Harper's Bazaar* of 1934, 'Vionnet opened on the dot with her phenomenal 1880 models cut with a modern dash ... as a result Vionnet stands today ... not for self-effacing crêpe de Chine but for conspicuous stiff bustles, picture dresses and triumphs in taffeta.' This was so at odds with her usual style that it was obviously news, and indeed her version of the bustle as a dashing bow and her masterful forcing of taffeta into a draped hour-glass shape were certainly 'cut with a modern dash'.

Within a year or two, however, she had apparently reverted to 'self-effacing crêpe de Chine' and soft silk, which she handled as if the stuff were molten. She veered from daring bare-backed dresses held up only by thin crossed straps, to totally covered-up dinner dresses which only that famous cut could have achieved. By 1938, for evening, drapery was confined to the bodice above skirts that were miracles of clinging cut. In 1939, just before closing down, she designed a dramatic fur jacket with a cloth back – which proves a remark she made to Bernard Nevill: 'I never once set in a sleeve.' It was a bravura achievement in fur.

There is an extraordinary affinity between Vionnet and Grès (before the war known as Alix). The resemblances are many: Grès, too, uses double-width fabric, although her favoured material is jersey – wool for day, silk for night. Drapery is her forte, too, but based on a different principle. Her great classic dresses call forth, like those of Vionnet, similes to Greek sculpture. Like Vionnet, Grès shows her clothes without benefit of accessories in equally-unadorned salons. Bettina Ballard found Vionnet's mannequins 'very tall, impolite, hardly deigning to open their coats to show the dresses'. Grès's are of assorted sizes but equally disdainful of their audience. Grès, years later in 1958, also had a flirtation with swagged taffeta, but she, like Vionnet, will be remembered not for the exceptions to her classic rule but for the superb draped dresses with their timeless purity and nobility.

Unfortunately, those who knew Vionnet seem only to have met her in her later years. Sir Cecil Beaton describes her as '...wearing somewhat masculine clothes and a trilby hat'. To Bettina Ballard she looked like 'someone's governess ... in her neat tailored suit and bowler hat.' She apparently had a weakness for men's hats, for another observer reports seeing her wearing a top hat with a veil. Sir Cecil Beaton saw her as 'a parrot-like little woman with a shock of white hair ...' Bernard Nevill thought her 'bird-like'. Actually, earlier photographs of about 1924 show her to have had a charming soft face, prematurely white hair and a small, somewhat beaky nose. Celia Bértin describes her as 'short, with small light-coloured eyes in a long thin face ...' with 'small delicate hands with extraordinary fine fingers'. Vionnet herself said, 'I was always small, and I hate small women.' Chanel could not imagine anyone not wanting to wear what she wore herself. Vionnet, on the other hand, only liked to dress tall, beautiful women.

Madeleine Vionnet had what seems to have been a rather sad childhood. Born at Aubervilliers in the Jura (exactly when is the usual puzzle), she was deserted by her mother when she was three. As her father, a tax collector, probably could not cope, she was sent to school at an early age where she did very well but was soon, at the age of twelve, apprenticed to a local dressmaker. At sixteen she left Aubervilliers for Paris, where she got a job at a small firm in the Rue de la Paix. She married at eighteen and had one child who died. The following year her marriage failed too, and the next she went to London, where she found a job in the tailoring workroom of Kate Reilly. There she stayed for five years, learning English as well as tailoring.

Her career really began when she returned to Paris and at the age of twenty-five found a job with the Callot Soeurs where, before long, she was assigned to make *toiles* for one of the sisters, Madame Gerber, who made the models – to Vionnet 'a great artist'. It is curious that at the Callot Soeurs – who were known for their elaboration, from lace, for which Proust found they went in too freely, through incredibly ornate Chinese embroideries to repoussé roses – that Vionnet got the idea, as she told Bernard Nevill, of 'how to discard'. On second thoughts, it might have been *because* they never did.

Anyway, in 1907 she left to go to Doucet. It was at Doucet that year that she first expressed her idea of freedom – freedom from corsets, 'presenting mannequins', as she said, 'for the first time in bare feet and sandals and in their own skins.' She had already freed necks from the high whalebone-stiffened constricting collars as early as 1901. Alison Settle recalled seeing a sketch of a model from 'Madame Vionnet's Lingerie Collection' of that year, which had a deep cowl at the back, baring both nape and neck. The wide low neck was one of her innovations which became a characteristic of the 'Vionnet' blouse of 1927 – in white crêpe de Chine, the rectangle made shallower for day by a two-inch band joined to the blouse by faggotting, a motif repeated on the sleeves.

She stayed with Doucet for five years, then left to open on her own in the Rue de Rivoli. This was in 1912, and the First World War soon cut short her burgeoning success. She resuscitated her business after the Armistice, and as it improved and as her clientèle grew in importance, she took over the lease of a grand mansion in the Avenue Montaigne. At last she had a house worthy of her talent. Madge Garland describes the salons as 'large, beige, empty'. From these austere premises she produced what Christian Dior called her 'masterpieces'. Her own apartments were, however, as Lord Curzon described those of his wife, 'of unexampled splendour'.

The only dissenting voice in the chorus of praise comes from Bettina Ballard, formerly *Vogue*'s fashion editor, who found her in 1935 to have 'a pathological fear of being copied and a hatred for the press. . . . Fashion editors had to beg to be permitted to photograph a model.' Perhaps it was the memory of these frustrations that soured Mrs Ballard. She gives full marks to the magnificent gold lamé dress, at present in the costume Collection of the Metropolitan Museum of Art, New York, about which Madeleine Ginsburg writes that even today it has 'an archetypal sex appeal'. Unfortunately, Mrs Ballard and Horst, *Vogue*'s photographer, were given ten minutes to photograph it, and she concluded in 1960 that the 'Vionnet nostalgia is more sentimental than practical'. This is one of Mrs Ballard's few failures of judgement. 'They remember me,' Vionnet stated to *Women's Wear Daily* in 1969, and they do today.

As she had enjoyed over-dressing the actress, Cécile Sorel, Vionnet probably might have been amused that her bias-cut white satin dresses had inspired Adrian in the early Thirties to design the slinky costumes which became a hallmark of Jean Harlow – an archetypal sexpot, if Mrs Ginsburg will forgive me.

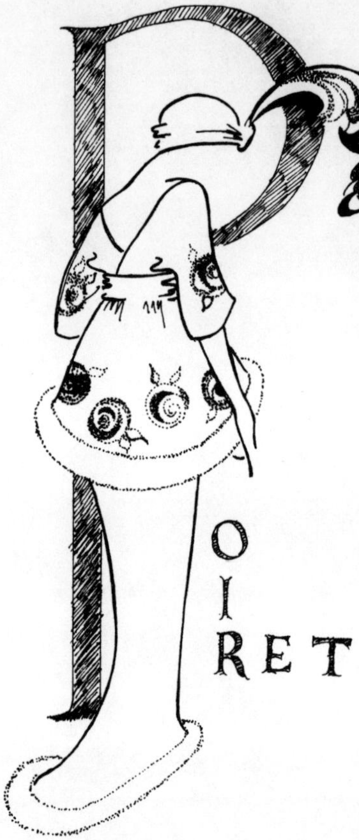
POIRET

PAUL POIRET

1879–1944

Maker of Dreams

Whatever one may think of Poiret now, he was in his time indisputably an arbiter, a name so magic that it survives today. Adventurous, often ridiculous and outrageous, always courageous, he could extricate the twentieth-century woman from her nineteenth-century carapace of whalebone and padding – and then smother her in exotic fantasies, free her body and hobble her ankles. He was a romantic escapist – one of the first; who but a romantic would have taken on the equally extravagant fantasist, Erté?

A native Parisian (he was born near the old Les Halles), Poiret started his career at the age of eighteen selling sketches. This was a path many were to follow, but he started at the top with Madame Chéruit, whose House was then one of the leading Houses in Paris. He was soon spotted by Jacques Doucet, who in 1896 took him on and allowed Poiret's innovative talents to emerge. Although he was only with Doucet briefly – about two years – this association must have influenced him, for Doucet, who had inherited a family business in the Rue de la Paix which he had radically changed until it rivalled that of Worth, was a remarkable man. He was distinguished in manner and mind; his interests went, as Poiret's were to go, beyond the confines of clothes. First attracted by the eighteenth century in painting and furniture, he formed a collection which he later sold when he became a connoisseur of contemporary French artists – Monet, Manet, Cézanne, Dégas, Le Douanier Rousseau, Braque and Picasso. It fetched, it is said, twenty million gold francs. His later collection was also sold for a handsome profit. (His Picasso, *Les Demoiselles d'Avignon* of 1907, which he acquired from the artist at the urging of the writers Louis Aragon and André Breton, now hangs in the Museum of Modern Art, New York.) Obviously working for such a man was an education in itself, and to be on the Rue de la Paix as well, about which it used to be said that if one sat long enough at the Café de la Paix all the world passed by, was added bliss.

Doucet, for all his cultivation, was not an innovator. He did not attempt to change the course of fashion; he simply softened it to make women look prettier. For them he made seductive dresses, often of fine lace, replete with flattering ruffles, flounces and ribbons. With the disappearance of a Court, fashion was led by actresses and *demi-mondaines*, and Doucet dressed both the leading ladies of the stage, Duse and Réjane.

Despite Poiret's youth, Doucet gave him his head and allowed him to design for Réjane (for whom as 'Zaza' he designed a dramatic coat which stopped the show) and even for the Divine Sarah for whom he did the costumes for *L'Aiglon*, from the photograph an empty joy. Unfortunately, Bernhardt was less than divine to Poiret, demanding his dismissal because of an overheard indiscreet remark. At this time Poiret was twenty-one, and due in any case to do his military service. When he re-emerged he joined the House of Worth. It was no small thing to have been employed by two of the most famous Houses in Paris, but Poiret was restless and anxious to be his own master. By 1903 he had acquired his own House, where his imaginative windows created a stir but failed to draw in the customers. His break came when Doucet, with noteworthy generosity, persuaded Réjane to give the young man a chance. With Réjane to promote it, the suit Poiret made for her in navy and scarlet was a success – and so was Poiret.

He became engaged that same year, acquiring a lovely fiancée who wore his most outrageous fantasies with grace and distinction. It was at the time of his marriage two years later that Poiret embarked upon what he called his 'revolution'.

The revolution was based upon the abolition of the corset. This created a sensation, but was he the first? There are other claimants for this honour, including Vionnet when she was working for Doucet, but that was not until 1907, after Poiret had left, and two years after he had persuaded Madame Poiret to discard hers. He was also to say that he invented the girdle (his was, according to Palmer

White, of rubber) and the brassière. Perhaps. Certainly, his slender captivating dresses, dropping from Empire waistlines, would have lost their delicious fluidity of line worn over the stiffly-boned corsets of 1911 or the hourglass corsets which preceded them.

Poiret also asserted that he was the first to use vibrant, primary colours for which he became known and which eclipsed the dainty 'sweet pea' colours, as Osbert Sitwell called them, beloved by the Edwardians. It is hard to believe that a man so aware of the art of his time could not have seen the famous Autumn Salon of 1905 which marked the debut of the group of painters known as Les Fauves, whose palette his colours reflected. As for the gentle, unconfined line, Geoffrey Squire has pointed out that soft, flowing dresses were being designed in Vienna by the artist Gustav Klimt, and Poiret often visited Vienna, then a fashion centre. As for the Ballets Russes, their first season in 1909 in Paris was the sensation of Europe, and the designs of Bakst and Benois are dangerously near the Orientalism that overtook Poiret. Yet all that his biographer, Palmer White, has to say about their influence on Poiret is that in 1909 Poiret, on a visit to London, went to the Victoria and Albert Museum where his eye was caught by the Indian turbans, especially those sprouting aigrettes. He was so enchanted by their possibilities that he sent to Paris for his milliner to come over and make *toiles* of them. 'It must also be said', Palmer White adds, 'that the turbans designed by Bakst to accompany the costumes of the dancers in certain of the Ballets Russes did much to reinforce the vogue launched by Poiret.' It is difficult to accept that *Schehérazade* had nothing to do with the barbaric splendour that pervaded his clothes, his salon, and his own legendary fancy dress parties.

However, it is, sadly, unimportant who did what first. What is important is who understood it best, interpreted it most powerfully, and expressed it most personally – and that person was Paul Poiret. He reigned supreme, and when with careless contradiction, having freed the body, he proceeded in 1910 to design the hobble skirt – a skirt which so shackled the ankles that it was practically impossible to walk – women everywhere could not wait to inch along like high-born Chinese ladies with bound feet, and presumably to conduct their lives on the level.

That was not the only sensation Poiret caused in London. Doris Langley Moore recalls seeing a hobble-skirted lady cause a near-riot on a London street in 1911. The irrepressible Margot Asquith, wife of the Liberal prime minister, had seen his collection in Paris and was so thrilled with it that she invited him to show it in London at one of her parties. This aroused the chauvinism of the British Press, who christened the Prime Minister's residence '10 Gowning Street' and made things pretty uncomfortable for poor Mr Asquith. Poiret was not pleased either. 'English women . . .', he wrote to his wife, 'look at a gown and exclaim as they swoon away in rapture, "Oh! Charming! Delicious! But whatever is it for? Tea, dinner, the opera?"' Poiret was furious, but many years later Mainbocher was to say, 'The worst thing a designer can hear is a client asking "When would I wear that?"' To Poiret, practicality was a dirty word.

Logic was not his forte. To Poiret life was a stage, and for it he designed costumes. It was not for nothing that he actually did design for the theatre; nor is it surprising that Erté entered fashion by way of Poiret's atelier. Poiret devised every kind of innovation: tunics of all kinds, the most spectacular, short ones like lampshades. The first of these was designed as a costume for his wife to wear at his famous 1002nd Night fancy dress party, at which he received his guests seated on a throne like an Eastern potentate, resplendent in fur-trimmed caftan and jewelled turban. His wife was imprisoned in a cage of gold, from which, when the guests arrived, Poiret released her. Her escape, her lampshade tunic swinging over full pantaloons caught at her delicate ankles, on her small turbanned head a towering aigrette, has been immortalized by the flattering pen of Georges Lepape. The costume was subsequently adapted for a play. *The Minaret*, and then by popular demand incorporated into his collections. Alas, the bird was eventually to fly away from her gilded cage for good, leaving Poiret desolate.

But at tunic time Poiret was monarch of all he surveyed, and his collections were fairy-tale processions. Besides the head-hugging aigretted turbans, pantaloons and Minaret tunics, he showed Turkish trousers and harem skirts. Huge tassels swung from his narrow high-waisted corded belts; fur-banded hems and cuffs on his simple dresses as well as on his sumptuous cloaks, wide at the top, tapering towards the toes and, like his evening dresses, richly-embroidered in gold or silver or glittering with beads. He added rare and exotic brocades and was the first to use fur as a fabric.

One of his most inspired ideas was to ask the artist, Paul Iribe, to design a publicity brochure for him, *Les Robes de Paul Poiret*, which appeared in 1909, and in 1911 to invite Georges Lepape to illustrate another, *Les Choses de Paul Poiret*. Both artists were to become the mainstay of *La Gazette du Bon Ton*, launched by Lucien Vogel in 1912. These young men, who understood Poiret's clothes, chronicled them with love. If the surviving originals of his extravaganzas look a bit tinselly today, they exist in their pristine charm in the illustrations of these two artists.

During all this time, as his success ballooned, Poiret was moving to larger premises, expanding, then extending them until he possessed three houses on three streets adjoining and adjacent to the original one – all in the Champs-Élysées area. In this, too, he was a pioneer, for this neighbourhood is now the heartland of couture. He was also expanding into other fields. 1911 was a bumper year; that year he worked on fabrics with Raoul Dufy and was the first couturier to launch and manufacture his own scents, the first of which he christened Rosine after his elder daughter. They were as carefully packaged as they were composed by still another of that year's enterprises: the new century had seen an upsurge of interest and activity in contemporary architecture and design, not only of interiors but of the decorative arts; with his wide-ranging interests, Poiret was fascinated by it all, and decided to set up his own atelier for the latter. This, which he called Martine after his second daughter, was soon turning out wallpaper, rugs, fabrics, furniture, objects, as well as the bottles and boxes for the Poiret scents.

A sketch of Poiret by Georges Lepape for the cover of his album shows him to have been a plump and peculiarly Parisian figure, looking more like a *boulevardier* than a dress designer. From his rotundity it is not surprising to learn that he was a president of 'Le Cent', a society of the hundred most discriminating gourmets of Paris. Nor is it surprising that the Oriental magnificence that made him turn his salon into a seraglio, his assistants into houris, persuaded him to give the fancy dress fêtes at which he and his wife were easily the fanciest of the dressers, should have inspired Diana Vreeland to dub him 'the Sultan of Fashion'.

It is ironic as well as tragic that this man, unique in the history of fashion, the first to foresee the post-war woman, should have been defeated by the war itself. Its aftermath brought a series of financial and personal difficulties for which the belated award of the *Légion d'Honneur* in 1944 did little to compensate. He eventually sank so low that Robert Piguet suggested to some of his colleagues that the Chambre Syndicate de la Couture Parisienne grant him a pension as some sort of recompense for all that he had done for the industry and its many ramifications, most of which he had introduced. The sum proposed was small enough, 1,000 francs a month; both Madame Lanvin and Madame Vionnet urged that this sum be doubled. It is sad to record that this much merited gesture was quashed by Jacques Worth.

Poiret died in 1944 at the age of sixty-five in, as Palmer White put it, 'poverty and oblivion'. It was a tragic end for the great exponent of luxury, in his time, as Mary Blume wrote in the *International Herald Tribune*, 'the epitome of that now faded word, Parisian'. Still, as long as the ideal of the thin woman persists, so will Poiret's name.

Chanel

GABRIELLE 'COCO' CHANEL

1883–1971

Magic of Self

During her long life Chanel wove such an elaborate tissue of lies about herself – where she was born, why she did something, what, when and where she did it and with whom – that hard facts are equally hard to come by. As Marcel Haedrich despairingly asked, 'How old was she when she was twenty?' She had even altered her birth certificate, lopping off ten years from her age and changing her place of birth from the Auvergne to 'near Marseilles'. It was Marcel Haedrich, however, the first to get a book off the ground after her death, who tracked down the real date of her birth from records at her real birthplace, Saumur. Thus all one can be certain of is that she was born in 1883 and died on 10 January 1971.

Chanel has left no written testimony, no letters, no papers: only a vast storehouse of anecdotes – some pure fiction, some with an apparent core of truth – which varied according to her mood, to her reaction to the person to whom she was talking, the impression she wished to make, and, as she had many Boswells, a plethora of quotations. The result is a kind of folklore, faithfully, if not accurately, repeated in every biography. Even the latest and most distinguished biographer, Edmonde Charles-Roux, former editor of French *Vogue* and winner of the Prix Goncourt, was forced, according to Philippa Toomey reviewing her book in *The Times*, 'to embroider, to assume, to speculate...' Chanel was creating a legend while she lived, a legend so powerful that it has survived her death.

If proof of this were needed, the sale of her personal effects – the clothes patently well-worn and dating only from her come-back in 1954, the Jewellery fake – which took place at Christie's London auction house on 2 December 1978, just slightly less than eight years after her death, provides it. One might have thought with Karl Lagerfeld, French ready-to-wear designer quoted in the *Sunday Times*, that the clothes were 'too recently *démodé*', that it was 'too soon for nostalgia'. But one would have been wrong, as was M.

Lagerfeld. Another quote, this time from Chanel herself, explains why. It was used with other of her pungent maxims, recollected and collected by her staunch admirer, Hervé Mille, in the foreword of the catalogue of the sale: *'Je n'aime pas que l'on parle de la mode Chanel. Chanel, c'est un style. Le mode se démode. Le style jamais.'* It was for the Chanel style that the 119 lots fetched the amazing total of £68, 655. Museums and private collectors competed for the serene simplicity of the clothes, shown with her characteristic accessories – the black-tipped sling-back slippers, the masses of gilt chains, the mean little fur tippets ('Fur is for inside,' she said), the pussy-cat bows, the quilted bags swinging from gilt chains, the artificial gardenia buttonholes ('Imagine wearing something that dies. If I wear a flower, it's an artificial one'). And especially her costume jewellery. The costume jewellery was sold separately. Although each item was meticulously catalogued as 'simulated' (stones) and 'metal' (settings), they went for Cartier prices – one brooch alone fetching £1,600, while the whole 44 lots realized £21,995. This would have been gratifying to the woman who invented fashion jewellery by reproducing her own magnificent collection of real jewels (said to have been given her by one of her lovers, Prince Dmitri of Russia), so that, as she said, 'Women can wear fortunes that cost nothing.' Well, not quite nothing.

Out of the miasma of contradictions an outline emerges. From humble beginnings, an orphan of doubtful parentage, Chanel attracted the attention of a dashing officer, Étienne Balsan, and soon came under his protection (or as Mlle Charles-Roux puts it, became his *irregulière*.) As she had learned to sew at the orphanage (a fact she later denied), besides teaching her to become a superb horsewoman, he set her up in a hat shop in Compiègne. He also, mistakenly as it turned out, introduced her to an English friend, Boy Capel, with whom she fell in love. They made an uncomfortable-sounding threesome – a sort of premature Design for Living – until Balsan tired of the situation and went off.

Now facts begin to shimmer in the golden haze of the Riviera sun in the last carefree days of the Belle Epoque: it was either at Deauville or Biarritz (you can take your choice) that she and Capel in 1910 (or was it 1914?) led the traditional, idyllic, smart resort life of which the ingredients were love, yachting, polo and pleasure. Observing how awkwardly skirts behaved when the wearers clambered up and down the boarding ladders of yachts, she adopted a pair of sailor's pants. She took over as well their pea jackets, striped maillots and berets – and remained faithful to the latter (with variations) for nearly thirty years, replacing them with the equally nautical *canotier* (boater to the British, sailor-hat to the Americans). She also remained faithful to navy blue and opened her first collection after her come-back in 1954 with a navy jersey suit topped by a navy straw sailor-hat – almost identical with an outfit she had shown before the war.

Watching polo, she picked up a man's polo sweater and sashed it with a kerchief. When she found all these casual improvizations being copied slavishly by the smart watering-place world, she opened a shop with Capel's backing to sell what she had been giving away. She also discovered her greatest asset: that she was one of nature's arbiters – all she had to do was be herself, wear what she liked to wear, and women would follow her.

Another of Chanel's maxims quoted by M. Mille – *'Le Schehérazade c'est facile. Une petite robe noir c'est difficile'* – contemptuously annihilated the fading fantasies of Poiret and revealed the secret of her success. It was ungrateful to Poiret, who had paved the way for her by abolishing the corset as far back as 1906 and cropping his models' hair in 1908. (Chanel did not cut hers until 1917, and when she did it was with a cock-and-bull story about her long hair being scorched by a gas-burner.) He had also been the first couturier to launch his own scent (the famous Chanel 5 did not appear until 1923) and the first to appreciate the Ballets Russes. It was not until 1917, when Chanel had met Misia Sert (whom Paul Morand called 'a collector of geniuses', and to whom Chanel owed her education in the arts and her acquaintance with the artists), that Chanel discovered the lure of the Ballets Russes. She, unlike Poiret, knew instinctively that the stage was where these glorious barbaric costumes and colours belonged, and that they were not to be confused with fashion. With Poiret's (and Vionnet's) help women's bodies had been freed. The war had freed the women themselves, and it was this independence that Chanel intuitively realized because she herself epitomized it.

When in 1919 after the First World War she re-opened her House in the Rue Cambon (she had first opened it in 1914 and, according to Claude Ballien, had 'almost felt that the war had broken out to spite her'), Chanel rode to fame on that 'little black dress'. Understanding the wish for ease and comfort and simplicity after the last voluptuous extravagance of the Second Empire, she took what had been considered 'poor' fabrics, like jersey and velveteen, and upgraded them. She put women into a uniform of loose cardigans, soft jumpers and easy pleated skirts.

Poor Poiret, who moaned with rueful humour, 'We ought to have been on our guard against that boyish head. It was going to give us every kind of shock and produce, out of its little conjurer's hat, gowns and coiffures and sweaters and jewels and boutiques.' His catalogue was incomplete. It was not only 'gowns and sweaters' that Chanel produced. If it is true that it was at Cannes in 1922 that she unveiled the sunburn she had accidentally acquired on a yachting trip, she was the first to show that brown is beautiful. She invented a new stance to go with that 'boyish head': hip thrust forward and hands thrust deep in the pockets which she had filched from men along with their trousers, for as women had taken over men's jobs in the war, she took over and transformed their clothes. From her nephew she borrowed his English blazer. From men she adopted their cuffed shirts – and cuff-links. Her turned-back jacket cuffs, which showed these off so well, she is said to have copied from a mannerism of Jean Cocteau. She gave birth to the *Garçonne* look but feminized hers by turning neckties into pussy-cat bows, tying a ribbon around her short hair or placing a fake flower or two on top.

As Coco Chanel she was famous; she was fêted. The openings of her collections were like smart *vernissages*, and at them she always sat at the top of the curving mirrored stairs, the steps below occupied by artists like Cocteau, Stravinsky, Picasso, Bébé Berand .... After her return in 1954 the occupants of these favoured seats were more apt to be important buyers and representatives of *Women's Wear Daily*.

She did not, of course, have the world of fashion to herself; there were other successful couturiers, but she seemed to consider them interlopers on her territory. And she fought them bitterly. She tolerated the elegant English Molyneux and Creed, the soft-spoken American Mainbocher, but Patou was an enemy. Schiaparelli, whom she dismissed as 'that Italian artist who makes dresses' was another. Feuding with her colleagues was a favourite pastime which she continued after her come-back. Two couturiers became her pet targets – Jacques Heim, then President of the Chambre Syndicale de la Couture Parisienne, and the aristocratic Antonio del Castillo – and with petty spite, she timed her openings to coincide with theirs, presenting the press with a pretty problem, for she did not welcome substitutes for the top dog of any publication.

Although Chanel left few if any scraps of paper, there exist innumerable photographs, snapshots and sketches. These show her never to have been beautiful in a classic sense. From them spring a gamine gaiety, a provocative, impudent independence. In a much-quoted phrase, Cocteau called her 'a little black swan', to which Edmonde Charles-Roux adds Colette's retort, 'with the heart of a little black bull'. In old age Chanel was more like a black (and not so little) monkey.

Her loves were many, and just as Brummell's friendship with the Prince of Wales established him, and the patronage of the Empress

Eugénie had propelled Worth into the great world, Chanel's much-touted affairs with Prince Dmitri of Russia and the Duke of Westminster did not harm her. It is clear from the remark which she made in differing ways over and over again to friends and interviewers that 'a woman needs to be caressed from her head to her toes', that physical love was as necessary to her as water to a flower. So other lovers succeeded these, more talented if less exalted – the artist Paul Iribe and poet Pierre Reverdy, introduced to her by Misia Sert, through whom she had also met Picasso.

Chanel's empire expanded from one to three Houses, and ultimately, it is variously estimated, to five or eight Houses in the Rue Cambon. She was dressing the world, not only from her Couture House but through the millions of copies that were made of her clothes. This she never minded, indeed positively welcomed, either before or after her come-back. She knew imitation to be the visible sign of success and was always shrewdly aware that a copy can only be a copy. In the era of drawing-room comedies, she also dressed actresses like Ina Claire, who, Carmel Snow said, 'really launched Chanel in America by wearing her clothes on the stage', and Florence Vidor. She designed for films and the ballet.

For the Ballets Russes, Chanel was invited by Diaghilev to design the costumes of *Le Train Bleu*. The scenario was by Jean Cocteau and was intended as a satire on the passengers of this glamorous train, typical Chanel customers. Picasso provided the curtain, for the sets Diaghilev chose a sculptor, Henri Laurens, and for the choreography, Bronislava Nijinska, Nijinsky's sister, who had worked with Diaghilev on such distinguished ballets as *Les Noces* and *Les Biches*. One of Chanel's original costumes for *Le Train Bleu* was sold on 14 June 1967 at Sotheby's in the first sale of costumes of the Ballets Russes, when for the first time in auction history these were modelled by real dancers, the students of the Royal Ballet School. The costume was a loosely hand-knit bathing-suit, a long top over shorts. Dame Ninette de Valois, who wore the costume in the original production, recalls Chanel at the dress rehearsal: 'She snapped, "Those girls look awful, all in beige, so unbecoming. We must find something different," so she swept us off to her salon and made us try on all the bathing-suits in her collection to find two that would do.'

Chanel may have been the first to display a suntan at Cannes in 1922, but surely it was her collaboration with Diaghilev on *Le Train Bleu* in 1924 which started the rage. Chanel's bathing-suits became the latest thing to wear and Deauville the smartest place to wear them. Diaghilev himself described the impact of the ballet:

> ... the first point about *Le Train Bleu* is that there is no blue train in it. This being the age of speed [sic], it has already reached its destination and disembarked its passengers. These are to be seen on a beach which does not exist, in front of a casino which exists still less. Overhead passes an aeroplane which you cannot see. And the plot represents nothing. Yet when it was presented for the first time in Paris, everybody was unaccountably seized with the desire to take the Blue Train to Deauville and perform refreshing exercises.

All over the Western world women who had been preserving their white skins as the *sine qua non* of beauty now worked equally hard at toasting themselves a golden brown. So one must conclude that Chanel shares the honours of introducing a new and lasting fashion with Diaghilev and *Le Train Bleu*. This may be why in later life she tended to brush off this episode.

Before *Le Train Bleu* Chanel had designed costumes for *Antigone* as translated (freely) by Cocteau. The sets were by Picasso, the music by Honegger. Edmonde Charles-Roux quotes Cocteau as telling the press, 'I asked Mademoiselle Chanel for the costumes because she is the greatest designer of our day and I do not see Oedipus's daughters badly dressed.' In 1931 Chanel extended her horizons still further; she went to Hollywood at the invitation of Sam Goldwyn and with the lure of a contract said to be for one million dollars. Chanel was to go to Hollywood twice a year. It had been Goldwyn's idea that she would dress his stars on and off the screen. This plan did not go down well with the stars, and in the end Chanel costumed only three films, all in 1931: *Tonight or Never* with the young Gloria Swanson, *Palmy Days* with Eddie Cantor and Charlotte Greenwood and *The Greeks Had a Word for It* with Ina Claire. As far as Chanel was concerned, that was it; she left Hollywood, and Metro-Goldwyn-Mayer was short-changed.

Figures are nearly always misleading, especially hers, but one can accept the assertion that by 1938 she had 4,000 employees and was selling throughout Europe, the United States of America, South America (all those rich Brazilians and Argentinians) and the Middle East. Her jewellery, of which the elegant Count Étienne de Beaumont was in charge from the early Twenties (joined in 1932 by the equally elegant Duca di Verdura), was also a sell-out, but her perfumes, with Chanel 5 as the star turn, were the real sources of her wealth.

Chapter One of Chanel's success closed with the Second World War. 'The first war made me. In 1919 I woke up famous,' she exclaimed joyously. In the intervening twenty years she had weathered the seismographic changes endemic to fashion with her usual moderation. In 1930, for example, when, after three years of dithering, skirts finally fell and waistlines rose spelling the end of her Garçonne look, she followed suit but resisted the extremes of her fellows. She was also to survive the mini and the midi, only remarking that the length of the skirt should depend on the length of the leg. She was still Chanel. But the Second World War defeated her. She closed her House in 1939 and holed up in her apartment at the Ritz. Not only did she opt out of the war, but she also took a German lover, well-born but still the enemy. Chanel's biographers seem to write with their pens dipped in treacle, and it is amusing to watch them attempt to sugar-coat this unpalatable pill. It was whispered that her return had been engineered by the people who made the scents which had made her fortune. They thought they needed her name and the glamour of her House to revivify their sales after the war – a story she strenuously denied. She remained in seclusion until 1954 when she electrified Paris by announcing her come-back.

Once again her timing was perfect. She had said of the early years, 'My time was ready for me, waiting. All I had to do was come on the scene.' In 1954, time was not exactly waiting for her, but she chose the right moment for her re-emergence. Nine years after the war was about the right length of time to let wartime passions spend themselves. In 1946 everyone in Paris had called everyone else a 'collabo' (collaborator). By 1954 the epithet had worn thin with such lavish and indiscriminate use. But even more importantly the influence of Christian Dior's New Look was waning; after a passionate love affair with its super-femininity women were tiring of its constriction. They were, although they did not at once realize it, ready for Chanel's unfettered ease.

Her first collection was received with an icy lack of enthusiasm by the Press – hard to understand when one looks at the adorable little navy suits, their crisp white shirts bowtied, the brimmed sailor-hats tilted back to the pre-'Tom Jones' bows holding the hair. By 1957 her soft suits of quilted English (Linton) tweed, bound in contrasting braid, their cardigan jackets jewel-buttoned and lined in delicate silks to match their shirts, exemplified the same love of piquant contrast she showed when she flung her priceless pearls over a plain black sweater. These and their matching coats were a success crazy. By 1962 they were the most copied suits and coats in the Western World, as were her short tailored black velvet and brocade theatre suits. She never repeated the romantic ruffled and sequinned evening dresses of the Thirties.

After the tremendous success of these clothes, she sensibly stuck to her last. Although fashion journalists began to dismiss her collection as 'the mixture as before', this was not true. As the *Sunday Times* put it on 8 April 1962: '... although they shared certain similarities, there are artful differences, just as at her collections the seeing eye can discover the subtle changes that mark her progression season by season.' On the same page the newspaper showed the first photograph of the latest version of her famous sling-back shoe in beige satin, tipped in black kid, made for her by Massaro, the strap, cut in one with the upper, swirling round the ankle to end just in front of the stiletto heel.

Still, Chanel never regained her domination of the Paris scene. Although her hated rival, Schiaparelli, closed her House in 1954, Jacques Fath died the same year and Dior was to die three years after, the magic of his name enabled the House of Dior to continue to flourish, first with Yves Saint Laurent, then with Marc Bohan. The House of Lanvin also continued with Castillo, followed by Jules François Crahay, who was replaced at the durable Nina Ricci by Gérard Pipart. With Dior's death the unapproachable Balenciaga led the field, while the serene and even more mysterious Grès went her own way, as did Balmain. New talents were crowding in: Givenchy, Cardin, Courrèges and Yves Saint Laurent, on his own since 1962, and on whose slim shoulders the mantle of leadership has now fallen. Of these Chanel was kindest – if that is the word – about the young Yves Saint Laurent, perhaps flattered by his manifest admiration for her, contenting herself with saying, as quoted by Felicity Green, that 'the poor boy might turn out all right if he copied me and cut his hair'. It is not known if this was before or after he evinced his admiration by dedicating a collection to her – *'Homage à Chanel'* – in which he did indeed copy her in a different way, repeating her typical mannerisms, even down to the artificial gardenia on the lapel. But he did not cut his hair.

In their wake came the YéYé group led by Féraud. And from across the Channel, Mary Quant was making her mini mark. Although Chanel fulminated against them, 31 Rue Cambon rocked gently with the Nouvelle Vague. Chanel's skirts rose and fell almost imperceptibly. Perhaps it was only coincidence that in 1964, the year of Courrèges's great success with trouser-suits, Chanel combined her first love with her last, showing navy flap-fronted sailor pants with her typical cardigan jacket. Whatever she inhaled was exhaled in her own smoke rings.

But despite the competition Chanel possessed a unique asset: her age. Longevity is a virtue in itself, especially to the French. Think of Ninon de L'Enclos reputedly taking her last lover at ninety, of Mistinguett swinging her eighty-some-years-old legs from a crescent moon in revues. Chanel in her seventies was ripe for canonization. She had refused the *Légion d'Honneur* before the war because it had been given to other designers, but in 1957 she accepted the Neiman-Marcus Award and, even more unusually, went to Dallas to receive it. The mountain came to Mahomet, but grumbling all the way.

In 1969, after eleven years of patient persuasion, *Coco*, the musical of her life, finally opened on Broadway. Frederick Brisson, the producer, had first had the idea in 1958, the year when the Chanel look was reaching its second apogee. He offered her Alan Jay Lerner to do the book, André Previn the music. The stumbling-block was Mademoiselle, who thought only she should play herself. She scornfully rejected actress after actress, including Mr Brisson's wife, Rosalind Russell, about whom she was extremely offensive. Eventually, the three negotiators succeeded in coaxing Mademoiselle into accepting Katharine Hepburn. It was only when, breathing sighs of relief, they were descending the famous staircase that it occurred to all three of them that the Hepburn that the eternal Mademoiselle had thought they meant was Audrey.

Mr Brisson had asked Cecil Beaton to design the costumes. Poor Mr Beaton. If he had done nothing else to deserve the knighthood bestowed on him in 1972, he would have deserved it for this effort alone. He had to design 250, not costumes but clothes, which had to have the Chanel look – a look which bore her imprint so powerfully as to be always recognizable, but was, as he said at the time, essentially 'un-dramatic, un-theatre'. He had a foreboding that whatever he did would be wrong in her eyes. He was, alas, right. As she had thought that only she could play her part, she also thought that only she could design the clothes. In a huff, she refused to attend the opening.

What can one make of this extraordinary woman, who had raised egocentricity to an art, whose personal intransigence was matched by an artistic intransigence which allowed her to span a half-century of change without altering her basic concept of clothes? She was not a dictator; she was too clever for that. A general can only be a few steps ahead of his troops; Chanel was always in step with hers. Jealous, petty, shrewd, suspicious, she was still a Fashion Immortal – an accolade given her by the (London) *Sunday Times* in 1963. She refused to come to London to receive the Award for the same reason that she had refused the *Légion d'Honneur*. She did, however, accept the delivery of the Award itself, dismissing it as 'a pretty piece of crystal'.

Coda

If there has been any doubt that Chanel is an immortal, the success of her House today will dispel it. Immediately after her death, Gaston Berthelot, who had been in charge of Christian Dior New York, was given the task of carrying on in the Chanel tradition. It was not an easy task but one which M. Berthelot tackled manfully for several seasons. However, the real Chanel explosion was set off in 1977 with the decision to make Chanel ready-to-wear as well as couture. Philippe Guibourgé, fifteen years with Christian Dior-Paris, was appointed to design Chanel ready-to-wear for the American market. His brief was to keep the Chanel look, essential for its aficionadas, to keep it as young as its eternally-youthful original progenitor and to keep it in tune with the times. M. Guibourgé brought off this triple challenge with such bravura that within a year there were nineteen boutiques in major stores in major cities stretching across the USA from coast to coast and from north to south, as well as one in Canada. Europe followed suit as boutiques were opened in Belgium, Germany, Switzerland and France. Then came the Far East with Hong Kong and Japan. Last year, as part of a Chanel festival, a boutique was opened on the ground floor of the House of Chanel as well.

The couture – designed since 1974 by two of Chanel's assistants who had worked closely with her since 1956, Jean Cazaubon and Yvonne Dudel – dresses the leading ladies of the French government; Philippe Guibourgé's ready-to-wear dresses Chanel fans all over the world, including London – the latest boutique to be opened which will have a shop all to itself.

The Chanel suit has once more become a uniform. Chanel revived – and seemingly forever.

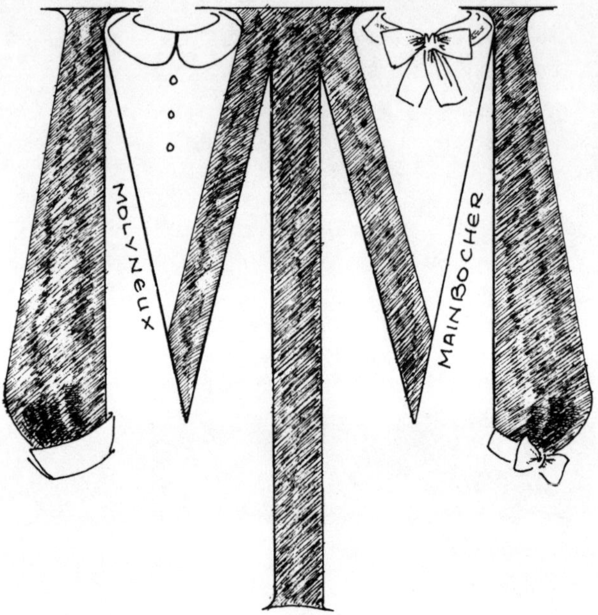
MOLYNEUX
MAINBOCHER

EDWARD MOLYNEUX

1891–1974

MAIN ROUSSEAU BOCHER 'MAINBOCHER'

1890–1976

The Two Gentlemen

It seems polite as well as politic to place the gentlemen between the two rival ladies – Chanel and Schiaparelli – although their (the gentlemen's) debuts were ten years apart. Captain Molyneux opened his salon at 14 Rue Royale in 1919: Mainbocher did not open his at 12 Avenue George V until 1929. Despite this difference in timing, the two were not unlike.

They were near in age, Mainbocher born in 1890 and Molyneux in 1891; both were foreigners (to chauvinistic French eyes), Molyneux English and Mainbocher, then Main Rousseau Bocher, American; both had been in the First World War, Molyneux on active service in a British regiment, Mainbocher serving in France as a volunteer in an American ambulance unit. Both were in the tradition of Patou (another of Chanel's hates) rather than Poiret, preferring to make clothes for ladies' rather than sensation's sake. (It was said of Mainbocher when he returned to New York, by Sally Kirkland, then fashion editor of *Life* magazine, that he could not only make a woman look like a lady but as if her mother had been a lady, too.) Both specialized in a seemingly easy simplicity although each had his own handwriting. Both were capable, in an understated manner, of innovations; Molyneux's printed dress and matching jacket were, for example, to become a uniform for summer town wear. And each was chosen to dress the bride on Royal occasions: Molyneux to make the wedding dress for Princess Marina when she married the Duke of Kent in 1934; Mainbocher to make the dress for Mrs Simpson's marriage to the Duke of Windsor in 1936.

In other ways they were very different; the Captain dashing and debonair, Mainbocher retiring and soft-spoken to the point of hush. It is characteristic of each that one should charge into battle, while the other succoured the wounded.

Molyneux

Edward Molyneux, after leaving Beaumont College (where Chanel also sent her nephew and which was described by *Vogue* in 1952 as 'a Roman Catholic school similar to Eton'), started his career as a sketcher for Lucile, the first British dressmaker to acquire an international reputation. His workroom was a perch on a landing at the turn of the curving staircase in her Hanover Square mansion. The landing had a vast drafty window which gave young Molyneux a perpetual cold in the head.

This was in 1911; in 1914 on the outbreak of war he joined up with the 9th Battalion Duke of Wellington's (West Riding) Regiment with which he served with distinction, was mentioned three times in dispatches, won the Military Cross and lost the sight of one eye. Hot on the heels of demobilization, he, as he put it, 'stormed the citadel of fashion' – Paris. This was a daring venture for his age and for an Englishman, but his auspices were as high as his courage, the newspapers reporting that his opening show had been attended by the British Ambassador, Lord Derby, making history by being the first ambassador 'to visit a dressmaker's salon on exhibition day'. Molyneux found himself at the age of twenty-eight an instant success, both professionally and socially.

Unusually good-looking, fair-haired and slender, with the loose-jointed grace of Fred Astaire, he epitomized the post-war scene in his private life as well as in the clothes he designed. The Twenties were dancing years, and with Elsa Maxwell, Molyneux opened a night club, 'Les Acacias', for which as dancing stars Molyneux hired Clifton Webb and Jenny, one of the famous Dolly sisters. For her, he, in an exaggerated Lucile mood, designed a cloak of white chiffon and feathers, eighteen feet long, which he covered with 5,000 real gardenias, its trailing length carried by two little black boys dressed as Nubian slaves. Later he and Miss Maxwell opened another night-club, 'Le Jardin de Ma Soeur', where the entertainers were Leonora Hughes with her partner, Maurice, and Josephine Baker. Molyneux's life became a merry-go-round on which he always caught the gold ring – with an Hispano Suiza, a yacht and a villa to show for it. He worked hard all day, gave extravagant parties or, equally extravagantly, gambled all night.

Pierre Balmain, hoping for a job, describes the Molyneux office at 5 Rue Royale, where Molyneux had moved in 1922, already needing larger premises. This address became associated with him throughout his designing life. 'Captain Molyneux', wrote Balmain, 'was standing in front of a blazing fire in a room with high windows, pearl-grey satin walls and mirror-covered pilasters. On the mirrored mantelpiece stood a rare Khmer head.' The whole salon, as Molyneux himself irreverently described it later, was 'all black and grey and white with plaster garlands and cupids' bottoms.' However, customers recall grey walls and carpets, matching satin-covered sofas and chairs. Staff, too, were dressed in grey with grey shoes to match. His much-photographed flat, to which at last Balmain was invited, with its mirrored walls painted by Drian with a flight of black and white storks, and dining-table of plate glass, was everything that was typical of the period. Balmain was awed by the luxury and, because of his ignorance of the language, by both Molyneux and his young assistant, John Cavanagh. 'It was', he wrote, 'rather like a Frenchman finding himself in an exclusive English club.'

Besides Jenny Dolly's fabulous cloak, admittedly exaggerated, photographs suggest that Molyneux's early efforts showed the influence of Lucile. Flowers appeared on shoulders, waists, or even appliquéd all over; ostrich feathers waved in fans or boas, and paillettes glittered. But by 1930 he had found the handwriting which became known as his. As Balmain wrote, '... the world's best-dressed women wore the inimitable two-pieces and tailored suits with pleated skirts, bearing the label Molyneux.... He always believed in an absolute simplicity that put duchesses into housemaids' dresses, and made them value the small white glazed collar more than their string of pearls.'

He had almost from the beginning dressed, besides his private clientèle, the stars of the British stage, from Gladys Cooper, for whose English rose delicacy he provided the early glamorous confectionery, to Gertrude Lawrence, in whose leggy grace he found the perfect exponent of his later style. His wide trousered lounging pyjamas, fur-collared and cuffed suits and bias-cut white satin evening dress for her in Nöel Coward's *Private Lives* in 1930 were the template for the decade. The three of them, Lawrence, Coward and Molyneux, became a real-life *Design for Living*, both on and off stage. Later, Molyneux was also to dress Lynn Fontanne, who starred in that play – everything was neatly tied up.

These plays were all, of course, in contemporary dress. Oddly enough, it was with his period costumes for *The Barretts of Wimpole Street* in 1933 that he exerted a triple influence on fashion: first immediate and then far-reaching. It was Piguet's recommendation that the young Balmain should see them that determined him to work with Molyneux; they initiated a romantic Victorian revival that affected even that purist, Vionnet, and their tiny waists and long bell-shaped skirts presaged the New Look. It is doubtful whether this play, even if Dior saw it, was in any way a direct inspiration, but it foretold a mood. However, it is true that Dior told Sir Cecil Beaton that 'it was certainly Molyneux's style that had most influenced him', and when he opened on his own his Egeria (if a designer can have an Egeria) was Madame Bricard, who had played this role for Molyneux. Stanley Marcus, no slouch at luxury, says that beside Madame Bricard both Madame de Pompadour and Marie Antoinette paled. When Mr Marcus, wishing to send her flowers to thank her for suggestions for his famous Neiman-Marcus Christmas catalogue, asked politely for the name of her favourite flower shop, Madame Bricard's reply was simple: 'Cartier.' It must have been the typical Molyneux elegant simplicity and economy of detail that Dior took as his model.

In 1932 Molyneux opened in London in a small house in Grosvenor Street, shortly afterwards moving to larger premises at

No. 48. Here he recreated his special ambience of grey: grey satin chairs and curtains, grey carpets – even the woodwork was painted grey, and the staff were dressed to match. As Sheila Wetton, his favourite mannequin and now a fashion editor of British *Vogue*, recalls: 'It was glamorous. Then, every country had a crowned head, and all their queens seemed to come to 48 Grosvenor Street.' It was there that Princess Marina's wedding dress was made. The Princess, with her sister, Princess Paul of Yugoslavia, had long been a client. For her, before and after her marriage to the Duke of Kent, he created soft dresses that set off her romantic beauty.

Molyneux oscillated between London and Paris until the Second World War, when, in June 1940, he escaped from France on a coal-barge. Even amid the soot, the overcrowding and confusion, his elegance was unimpaired. Every day at cocktail time his former batman and butler for twenty years always appeared, wearing his white coat and carrying a shaker of martinis. Back in London, Molyneux lived at Claridge's, fire-watching on the roof at night. To save petrol, he travelled by bicycle – a far cry from the Hispano Suiza.

Responding to a clarion call from the British Department of Overseas Trade, he established an export beach-head in the American market in 1941 and that same year joined a group of top British designers in sending a collection to South America. The next year he became a founder member of the new-born Incorporated Society of London Fashion Designers and subsequently its President. When he returned to Paris in 1945 the world of couture gave him a party to welcome him back to 5 Rue Royale. They were to give another party on a less joyous occasion – a farewell party in 1950 when because of failing sight he closed both his salons.

But Molyneux was not only a success in fashion; he had a Midas touch in other fields as well. He had always painted and collected paintings. His taste was so discriminating and his judgment so sound that his collections were sold *en bloc*. In 1933 he sold his collection of eighteenth century works of art for a fortune. In 1952 his collection of Impressionist paintings was exhibited at the National Gallery of Art in Washington, DC, and at the Museum of Modern Art in New York. It was subsequently sold to Mrs Ailsa Mellon Bruce for a reputed million dollars. Immediately after the showing of his first couture collection on his return to the Rue Royale in 1965, he flew to New York for an exhibition of his own paintings at the Hammer Gallery.

In 1951 after he had shut up shop – or, rather, shops – he built a house in Montego Bay, Jamaica, which he kept until 1959. One of the first to discover the delights of Jamaica, he was soon joined by Noël Coward and Ian Fleming. In 1956 he began building a house in Biot, Alpes Maritimes, the gardening heart of France where flowers are grown only for scent. He decided to specialize in carnations, soon built up a thriving business and acquired another fortune.

In 1963 he was persuaded to come to London for the first of the *Sunday Times*'s International Fashion Awards. This, he said, 'woke me from my dream'. He began contemplating a return to fashion which became a reality in 1965. Although he chose his old address, 5 Rue Royale (he considered five his lucky number), he did not attempt to reproduce the décor of his previous salon. 'I've gone off all that,' he said, and he chose champagne Japanese wallpaper and *tête de negre* carpets and, instead of the conventional fragile gilt chairs, 'modern Italian-type, as strong as possible', wood with rush seats. The only echoes of the Twenties were two mirrored walls.

Despite a team of talented young men, chief of whom was John Tullis, and despite the patronage of successive British Ambassadresses and the loyalty of former clients, it was impossible to re-establish the old Molyneux image. He found the jeans and boots 'all great fun', but, he added, 'nothing to do with chic.' Alas, it proved to be the new chic, and Molyneux gradually – like the fading smile of the Cheshire cat – retired, eventually moving to Monte Carlo, where he died in 1974 at the age of eighty-three. Perhaps he should not have been tempted back, for the magic of his name shone most brightly in the years up to 1950.

Mainbocher (Main Rousseau Bocher)

Oddly enough, it was Molyneux who, indirectly, set this Chicago-born designer on the road to becoming the first and, until now, the only American and, as far as is known, the only journalist to succeed in becoming a Paris couturier. Mainbocher, in Paris primarily to study voice, had had some success in New York with fashion sketches and one day approached the now established Captain Molyneux to show him some of his work. Molyneux was interested, though not to the point of purchase, but as Mainbocher was leaving, the directrice of the salon suggested that he show his sketches to the *Harper's Bazaar* Paris office. Mrs Chase, editor of *Vogue*, whose rivalry with this publication was as fierce as that between Chanel and Schiaparelli, is vague about these days, and skips lightly to his appointment as fashion editor of French *Vogue* in 1922 without credit to Carmel Snow (subsequently editor of *Harper's Bazaar* but then on *Vogue*) through whose perspicacity the transfer was effected. Mainbocher was to become editor of French *Vogue*, where he remained until the year he made his debut as a couturier.

As editor, he was a one-man band: editing, writing (he invented 'Vogue's Eye View') and drawing as well. His experience sketching had given him a sharp eye and an independent view. He did not wait, as was then the habit, to see what the buyers bought but published the clothes he liked. He has said that his main interest was in the look of the magazine, and, as well as selecting the right clothes, he looked about for the right photographers and illustrators. He encouraged Hoyningen-Huene, who had come to him to peddle some Man Ray photographs, to become a photographer himself; he encouraged Eric (Carl Erickson) to develop his much imitated but never equalled style. (Eric was to repay him by becoming the most perceptive portrayer of Mainbocher's work.)

In fashion, Mainbocher's taste was personal. In his subtle view Poiret was too theatrical; Chanel, too *dégagé*; Schiaparelli, too eccentric. His favourites were Vionnet, Augustabernard and Louiseboulanger. He paid the latter two the compliment of imitation when he struck out as a couturier by eliding his name too. What is curious is that this designer who dressed ladies as ladies should have also had an admiration for the *poules de luxe* who, as well as the aristocracy of birth and/or wealth, had since Worth been clients of couture. He had one particular favourite who 'won him', so he said, because it was the first time he had ever seen a chinchilla coat 'dragged across the floor'. He also saw the well-kept *demi-mondaine* at the races, where she wore 'sloppy hats and gloves a size too big. She was the epitome of chic.' None of the arrogant throwaway extravaganzas appeared in his own collections, except, perhaps, distilled into elegance as a reefer of gold lamé or a mink-lined shawl.

Mainbocher's debut in 1929, although not an instant money-spinner, was a *succès d'estime* and established his prestige. He kept a close eye on what clothes were worn and how and by whom through two of the beauties who had come to Paris as part of Patou's team of society models: Foxy Gwynn (later the Countess of Sefton) and Lillian Fisher. His success, though not immediate, showed a steady improvement, and by the approach of the war his staff had grown to 350. In 1936 he became internationally known when he was chosen by Mrs Simpson, whom he had dressed for some time, to make the dress for her marriage to the Duke of Windsor. The dress is now in the Costume Institute of the Metropolitan Museum of Art, New York. In a specially-dyed shade of blue which he christened 'Wallis' blue, it embodied one of his innovations – the wide inset corselet, one of the least happy of his inspirations and, unfortunately, one of the most copied. The Duchess was, according to Dale McConathy, a powerful influence. He admired her lack of self-deception about her looks, and her pin-neatness, her disciplined grooming, her liking for and ability to wear clothes of sophisticated simplicity suited and inspired him.

The war came at the height of his success, and in 1939 he bade farewell to his flower-filled salon with its Nymphenburg ornaments and zebra rugs, and returned to the land of his birth. In 1941, in his first premises on East 57th Street, he reproduced the quiet elegance of his Paris salon with beige walls, a slightly paler carpet and off-white curtains. Beneath a ceiling painted pale blue with floating white clouds, banquettes covered in coffee-coloured felt were set round the walls. The only touch of elaboration was the pair of eighteenth-century looking-glasses in rococo frames. This background suited Mainbocher at fifty, with his thatch of white hair, his benign intelligent face and his addiction to cashmere pullovers just visible under his jackets, as it must have suited him twelve years earlier, when he was dark-haired, slimmer and more conventionally dressed. He later moved to Fifth Avenue, where he reproduced the decor once more.

In Paris he had not eschewed drama, as a sketch of a magnificent floor-length coat of 1938, luxuriously fur-trimmed with a voluminous muff to match, shows. The dress beneath, of the same fabric as the coat, its fullness dropping from a wide-necked gathered top, presaged the Balenciaga sack of 1957 and could be worn today. It was in Paris, too, that he introduced the short evening dress, the strapless evening dress, and in 1939 the long dress with a late Victorian corsetted torso with cinched-in waist and bustle-like back drapery. That year he also designed a lace-up corset, memorably photographed in a Dali-esque manner by Horst. (Mainbocher subsequently sold the corset in 1940 to the corset firm of Warner Brothers; seven years later Warner Brothers in England were to make Dior's wasp-waisted guêpière.)

In New York, however, Mainbocher relinquished his nostalgia for Victoriana, although he held to his liking for the polonaise, on which he played cadenzas of his own composing. Chaste simplicity was the key word. Into his serene (and hushed) salon his models strolled in low-heeled black court shoes, wearing white gloves and flat bows in their hair, their only jewellery pearl earrings and a triple strand of pearls. As Sally Kirkland, then fashion editor of *Life*, put it, his collections were 'under-whelming'. As he himself put it, 'I dislike fashions that go off in your hands like fire-crackers,' and he added, 'High fashion is not for everybody; I don't think most people want to be white blackbirds.' Soon, as in Paris where his clients included Mrs Fellowes, Mme Patiño, Marie Laure, the Vicomtesse de Noailles and Lady Mendl, in New York his clientele embraced the shiny paper magazines' favourite beauties: Mrs William Paley, Mrs John Wilson, Mrs Winston Guest, Mrs Wyatt Cooper (Gloria Vanderbilt), Mrs Gilbert Miller and so on and so on. For these glossy clients he chose a direction which, although he may not have realized it, was in line with Chanel and Schiaparelli, neither of whom he approved. As Chanel had lifted jersey to a new level and Schiaparelli had promoted Viyella from the nursery (and as Claire McCardell in New York had transformed calico and denim), Mainbocher took knitted cardigans from the country club into the drawing-room by the skilful use of bead embroidery or by lining them with the same printed silk as the dress beneath. He gave a fresh meaning to naive fabrics like piqué and gingham. He liked the double possibilities of overskirts, the freedom of the sleeveless day dress which he invented, and the informality of the peasant-inspired so-called 'cocktail' apron, which he used to ring changes on his little, now dubbed 'basic', black dresses.

As well as grand ladies, and those who would be grand, Mainbocher also designed for the theatre, where he could express his sense of drama. Just as comfort – and the confidence that comes with it – was his primary concern for his customers, so it was in his clothes for actresses. Stars he dressed ranged from Irene Worth in *Tiny Alice* (Miss Worth chose Zandra Rhodes for the London production), to Lynn Fontanne and Ethel Merman. Perhaps his most famous costumes were for Mary Martin in *One Touch of Venus*, which he lined with pink silk. When the producer complained that these linings added to the cost and could not be seen anyway, Miss Martin replied, 'But *I* know they're there.' The luxury of linings and the ribbon Mainbocher tied around her long neck gave Miss Martin the glamour she had previously lacked.

Mainbocher closed his salon in 1971, and it is estimated that his surplus fabric – for fabric was his greatest luxury – was worth $100,000. He retired to Europe, where he alternated between Paris and Munich. It was in Munich that he died in December 1976, at the age of eighty-three.

What was this gentle man's special contribution? It was not only that he was a perfectionist, that he stood for that old-fashioned word 'refinement' in a period which was racing into vulgarity; it was not only his innovations, which by his own wish were never trumpeted, although the nipped waist pre-dated Dior, while the sleeveless dress is permanent. It was, I think, first, his attitude to his work. Chanel had said, 'Fashion is not an art, it is a business.' Mainbocher said, 'I do not believe dressmaking is an art, but I do think it is an important part of the art of living . . .' Second, it was his attitude toward his customers: 'No woman,' he said, 'should be forgotten. The woman with problems is entitled to just as good clothes as the fortunate woman who can wear anything. Cut should be helpful rather than demanding.' 'I have,' he added, 'no wish to dictate.' Perhaps that is why he always seemed to deliver his message in a whisper – not for him the shout.

chiaparelli

ELSA SCHIAPARELLI

1890–1973

Shocking

Perhaps the reason Chanel so hated Elsa Schiaparelli was not just because of her success – for although she did not equal Chanel in terms of sales and profits, she was certainly, by the Thirties, more talked about. When Chanel dismissed her as 'that Italian artist who makes dresses', there was a heavy load of envy implied by the word 'artist', for although Schiaparelli was herself only an amateur artist – she had dabbled in sculpture and painting – she came from a cultivated Roman family, her father a professor of Oriental languages, her uncle a distinguished astronomer. An affinity with artists came naturally to her. Unlike Chanel she needed no Misia Sert to act as go-between; she, too, had had to work for her success but in an even harder way, for she had no backers, and she had an adored daughter to support.

Marriage took her to New York; separation took her to Paris. *'Le sport'* had become the fashionable thing and with it a new interest in the previously dull sweater, and especially in those which were hand-knit. Once in Paris, Schiaparelli found an Armenian who could knit to her design, and she set up shop in her rooms on the Left Bank. These rooms became a Mecca for rich Americans who had heard of 'the little woman' who made such 'amusing' sweaters. Schiaparelli had invented the 'dressy' sweater; in 1927 she was to improve on this image when she created the first of a series of *trompe l'oeil* sweaters which were to become part of fashion history. Black and white has always been a basic Italian combination, and into a black sweater, Schiaparelli knitted in a white collar with what she called 'a large butterfly bow', like a child's naive drawing. Anita Loos, who looked a bit like Schiap, was one of the first to wear one.

Practically overnight she ceased to be a 'little woman' and became a Name. That year she moved to an attic in the Rue de la Paix, where she set up a workshop staffed by Armenian knitters – a sort of early Women's Home Industries project. Soon, having added to her range skirts and jackets to be worn with her sweaters, into which she incorporated the fashionable movements in art –

Cubism, Futurism, African Negro Art, as well as Surrealism – she was able to take over the whole house. It was from these premises that in 1931 she launched the wide, padded shoulders which, it is said, she took from British Guardsmen's greatcoats and which became her hallmark. These were not only to change fashion at the time but because of the war were, in a hideously-exaggerated form, to outlast their normal life expectancy.

At this point the seeker after truth finds himself in a maze which seems to obscure the history of contemporary fashion. Actually, the first shadow of the approaching confusion fell on the date of Schiaparelli's birth. Was it 1890 or 1896? As *The Times* delicately put it, 'her age was a subject on which she herself was reticent.' In this she was at one with Oscar Wilde's Lady Bracknell, who pronounced, 'No woman should ever be quite accurate about her age. It looks so calculating.' A solid fact is that she died in 1973. Less solid is the date of the watershed of her professional life, when she moved to the magnificent house in the Place Vendôme which had belonged to Mme Cheruit; it is given both as 1934 and 1935. The former seems more likely, as she is said to have opened her London House in 1934, and even to a woman of her dynamic energy the opening of two large Houses simultaneously would be an exhausting exercise. Nor is there agreement on from which premises she launched the clothes which were to change fashion, not only in their time but also as echoed today.

It does not really matter, for from whichever address there poured a continuous torrent of new ideas. Schiap herself was small, dark, completely Italian in her looks, and not at all beautiful. As Chanel had projected herself in creating the *garçonne*, Schiap projected herself as the *belle laide*. She made no concessions to prettiness. Where Chanel had given women casual ease, Schiaparelli gave them disciplined clothes: tight skirts and fitted, waisted jackets, immaculately-tailored (Diana Vreeland says her workrooms were among the best in Paris). Where Chanel had softened the ideas she filched from men's clothes, Schiaparelli exaggerated them; she even made her wide shoulders wider with sprays of gilded or glycerined coq feathers, emphasized them with elaborate embroideries, or soutache braid, which she revived. She invented the long (and demanding) evening suit, and her 'little black dresses' rivalled Chanel's.

The post-war mood was brittle and frenetic. To be sophisticated was the ideal, to be amused and to be shocked. Schiap knew how to amuse, loved to shock. She introduced the hot Italian pink which was to become so familiar after the war when Italian designers enlarged the fashion boundaries, called it 'shocking pink' and made it her own. She christened her scent 'Shocking', and had the bottle, a female torso with a heart on the left bossom, designed for her by the surrealist artist, Leonor Fini.

She was in fact far closer to Poiret than to Chanel, and, like Poiret's, many of her inventions seem today to be pure gimmickry, like the gloves imitating hands, complete with varnished nails – a typical Dali jape. Fortunately, she had the perfect clothes-horse for her most extravagant fancies in the Hon. Mrs Reginald Fellowes, born Princesse de Broglie. It was fashionable at the time for smart French women to be known by names like Norah, Cora, Jennie or Daisy, causing Nancy Mitford's Lady Montdore to grumble, 'Are all Frenchwomen called after English housemaids?' Mrs Fellowes, nothing if not fashionable, was known as Daisy. She wore with aplomb Schiaparelli's most outrageous jokes, hats in the shape of a shoe or a frilled lamb cutlet. Mrs Fellowes became so famous for these hats that one of them was included in a treasure hunt organized by Elsa Maxwell, and known then as a 'Scavanger party', along with such other items as a swan from the Bois de Boulogne and a cooked sausage. Mrs Fellowes's favourite Schiaparelli outfit most often noticed by English *Vogue* was a black dress with a sequin jacket and a green carnation (shades of Robert Hichens). *Vogue* seemed to think the dress may not have been the same one, which is likely, for as Mrs Fellowes always bought her jewellery in pairs, why not her dresses, too? Anyway, as Schiaparelli's *mannequin mondaine* (society model), she was probably dressed for free.

As Chanel had put her clients into uniform, so did Schiaparelli. Her handwriting was immediately identifiable which gave confidence like, as the advertisements used to say, a Bigelow on the floor or a Cadillac at the door. Also, just as it has been said that a man should always tell a pretty woman that she is clever and a plain one that she is pretty, pretty women enjoyed the challenge of looking a bit freakish, while plain ones enjoyed the unaccustomed pleasure of being noticed, and shy ones felt reassured when wearing an instant conversation piece.

While Schiaparelli kept her silhouette uncompromisingly strict, her trimmings were elaborate. Well before far-flung countries became the Mecca of couturiers in search of new ideas and long before ethnic became a fashion word, Schiaparelli Hester Stanhoped, absorbing details rather than whole costumes, colours like Tunisian blue and saffron yellow, exotic embroideries. She did not neglect contemporary artists. Where Chanel loved them as artists, Schiaparelli used them as designers. Christian Bérard designed the famous Medusa head in sparkling sequins for the back of a short evening cape; Jean Cocteau contributed a head with flowing hair for an evening cloak; Salvador Dali dreamed up a lobster print, as well as ideas for pockets like tiny drawers or letter boxes; Jean Hugo invented new buttons. Indeed, buttons, a neglected field, were given new life by Schiap: the famous jeweller, Jean Schlumberger, got his start inventing buttons for the boutique designed for her by Jean Michel Frank in 1935. If not the most important in Paris, it was, as Bettina Ballard wrote, certainly the most original and tempting with its sofa in the shape of a pair of bright red lips by Dali, and its straw figures on which were flung scarves and belts or hung with handbags or pinned with costume jewellery. The figures were also used to display the separates – a commonplace today but a fashion which she pioneered. It was these blouses and skirts that propelled Hubert de Givenchy into fashion.

Besides revitalizing the button, Schiaparelli experimented with other forms of fastenings. She was early (1930) in introducing the zipper into high fashion and, later, at the beginning of the war when materials were scarce, she used chains and dog-lead clips (Later Bonnie Cashin in America was to do the same for industrial hardware.) Schiaparelli was adventurous, too, in the use of synthetic fabrics, and as Chanel had lifted jersey into respectability as a high fashion fabric, Schiaparelli did the same for Viyella, a kind of British challis, previously restricted to the nursery set. Chanel had looked across the channel for her Linton tweed; Schiaparelli went further to find her tweeds in Skye and Ireland. She also liked 'dry' fabrics, crisp and textured.

Schiaparelli was a past mistress of publicity. She knew, in Cocteau's phrase, 'how far to go too far'. She was also a shrewd business woman. In her London House she introduced a very sensible financial device – for those who could afford it. A client worked out how much she could spend in a year and handed over that sum, for which she was allocated points – so many for an evening dress, so many for a cloak, or a suit, a coat or hat. Thus Schiaparelli was securely pre-financed, while her clients were amused, endlessly working out if their points were sufficient for the temptations proffered.

When war broke out, Schiaparelli was criticized, as was Mainbocher, for leaving France. According to Mrs Chase, Editor-in-chief of all the *Vogues*, she did not leave until the capitulation, although before that there was nothing for the couture to do – that is, those couturiers who were not already in the army. The materials that make beautiful clothes, from fabrics to buttons, were hard to obtain; tailors were called up. Again according to Mrs Chase, a fascinating group met at Mme Lanvin's in Bordeaux – Balenciaga, Molyneux, Patou, Heim, Piguet, Schiaparelli and

Lelong. There they heard the shattering news of France's capitulation. A decision was made. Molyneux, who was English, should return to London. Lelong was to stay and protect the remnants of the couture against the conquerors, a task he accomplished brilliantly, thwarting their plan to transport the couture lock, stock and barrel, to Berlin. Schiaparelli, who, it seems, had a contract for a lecture tour, was to make her way to America. It apparently made sense to Mrs Chase, but it does sound a bit feeble today. And perhaps it was a fatal decision, for although her loyal staff kept the House open and it survived for a short while after the war, and her scent continues, Schiaparelli never regained her position.

She left, however, a lasting legacy. As fashion was frozen during the war, Schiaparelli's wide padded shoulders lasted, not only during those years but, in America and particularly in Hollywood, into the Forties, their width exaggerated and the padding heightened. This peculiarly hideous fashion seems to have become a lasting legacy, cropping up periodically in Saint Laurent's collections, first in 1972 and, led by him again, in the Paris Collections of 1979. And not only the shoulders but the whole skinny, tight look of suits is reminiscent of Schiaparelli.

Would Schiaparelli be amused? One would hope so. 'Amusing' was her word, and it must be the height of amusement to be an arbiter of fashion in afterlife. Diana Vreeland has provided the best epitaph for this adventurous talent. 'She brought to the world of fashion,' wrote Mrs Vreeland in the catalogue of her first exhibition for the Costume Institute of the Metropolitan Museum of Art, 'daring, playfulness and fun.' To which one can only add audacity, originality and the courage of her most outrageous convictions.

DIOR

CHRISTIAN DIOR

1905–1957

Magic of Perfection

If the post-First World War was waiting for Chanel, the post-Second World War was positively aching for Dior. Paris was recovering from the humiliation of the capitulation and the hardships of the occupation and was still enjoying the euphoria of the liberation. The couture, with subsidies from an astute government, was emerging from the shadows of war with renewed brilliance. Most of the great names of the pre-war days were back designing with what seemed a new energy and zest. The roster included Lelong, Piguet, Patou, Paquin, Grès (before the war known as Alix), Dessès, Fath, Rochas, Lanvin, Nina Ricci, Schiaparelli (briefly) and Balenciaga. To this glittering galaxy were added two new names which were to become equally famous: Pierre Balmain, who had opened in 1946, and Christian Dior, who opened in 1947. Few centres have been so rich in talent or had so flourishing a couture. Buyers were beginning to flock in like hungry fowl pecking for seeds, starved for the fund of ideas, and, like the journalists, at last able to come to Paris again, reeling at the exquisite workmanship, the imaginative detail, the sumptuous luxury and sheer beauty of the clothes.

It was onto this crowded stage that Christian Dior leapt to instant stardom. With the backing of a rich cotton manufacturer, Marcel Boussac, 30 Avenue Montaigne was what Dior described as a 'small house' with 'neat, modest proportions, and an air of sober elegance'. It was perhaps not as magnificent as that of Jean Dessès, but Dior was right; it had elegance, with its unpretentious courtyard entrance, its handsome salon for which Victor Grandpierre created, wrote Dior, 'the "Helleu" atmosphere of my dreams, all in white and pearl grey, looking very Parisian with its crystal chandeliers and profusion of quintias palms . . .' The then small boutique was 'covered in toile de Jouy and scattered with hat-boxes . . .' – an inspiration of Christian Bérard's. It was not, however, the decor that excited – other Houses in Paris were equally beautiful – it was the collection. No one who was lucky enough to be present at this début will ever forget it.

The model girls entered the salon, their tiny hats by Maud et Nano tipped to one side, held on by veils caught under the chin, or else simply defying the laws of gravity. As Chanel had invented a stance, Dior had invented a walk, perilously back-tilted, which added to the arrogance with which they pirouetted in their calf-grazing, voluminous skirts (one contained eighty yards of fabric). It was not only the length (a foot or more from the ground) that excited; it was the contrast of the discipline of the fitted bodices with their tiny wasp waists and the billowing grace of the full skirts, the softly curved shoulders and the nonchalant back-dipping, open collars.

To English journalists in their sharp-shouldered (a legacy from Schiaparelli frozen by the war), skimpy fabric-rationed suits, this softness and fullness was, as one journalist put it, 'positively voluptuous'. All round the salon the overseas press could be spotted tugging at their skirts, trying vainly to inch them over their knees. The models, pushing, as Dior wrote, 'detachment to the point of insolence', swirled on contemptuously, their heavy skirts bowling over the standing ashtrays like ninepins. The New Look had been born – a look which was to change the shape of fashion, whose influence was to last nearly a decade and to make the name of its shy, unassuming designer world famous.

The word had spread about this new House before it had opened, in part due to the publicity skill of American Harrison Elliot, the charm of husky-voiced Suzanne Luling, the directrice, and the enthusiasm of Dior's great friends, society's pets, with naughty, Marie-Louise Bousquet and Christian (Bébé) Bérard. Paris buzzed, and even the taxi-drivers were agog to hear what this previously unknown designer had to show.

The traditional applause for the wedding dress which signals the end of each couture collection swelled into an ovation, with the audience calling for the designer who was routed out from the models' *cabine* and coaxed through the grey satin curtains to receive the cheers of the Press, the kisses of friends and the bursting of flashbulbs. This shy entrance and emotional reception survived all of Dior's collections and became a routine for those who followed. But for Christian Dior it was a 'supreme moment'. It was left to his friend Bébé Bérard to pronounce the perfect epilogue to this first great triumph, in an impromptu toast at a dinner given by Marie Louise Bousquet, to whom talent was almost as important as sex – well, not quite. 'My dear Christian,' Bérard said, 'savour this moment of happiness well, for it is unique in your career. Never again will success come to you so easily for tomorrow begins the anguish of living up to and, if possible, surpassing yourself.'

Of course Dior had had an apprenticeship, first with Robert Piguet and then with Lucien Lelong, but as he wrote in his beguiling autobiography *Dior by Dior*, 'I was only a designer who vanished from sight once my dresses had been created.' It has been stated that Lelong was not a designer himself; neither was Diaghilev a dancer, but each knew how to spot talent and to provide the climate for it to flower. It was from the spring-board of Lelong that both Balmain, who had come to him after five years at Molyneux, and Christian Dior leapt to fame. The two men became friends and talked of setting up on their own together, but in the end it was Balmain who took the first step, opening in 1946, a year before Dior. It is a truism that there is rarely a totally original idea in fashion. As Mainbocher once put it, 'I sniff the air.' In Balmain's first brief encounter with Piguet, Piguet had told him to be sure to see *The Barretts of Wimpole Street*, for which Molyneux had designed the costumes whose romantic Victorian crinolines Piguet thought a harbinger of a newer, softer look. This was in 1933. By 1938 both Molyneux and Mainbocher were showing fuller skirts, and the latter was even then adding decorative petticoats. In 1945 Balenciaga was tightening waists and rounding hips.

It was in the air and Dior sniffed it. As he had said to Cecil Beaton, whose vignette of Dior cannot be improved upon, 'Nothing is ever invented. You always start from something.' The something he sniffed was that women were tired of wartime uniforms and wartime restrictions. They were unconsciously ready for the intense femininity of Dior's clothes. In *The Blessing* Nancy Mitford – it could be with tongue in cheek – describes Madame Rocher at seventy exuding 'great billows of sex' in a dress with a dangerously low-cut bodice of 'pale blue glass bubbles embroidered on yellow silk; her pale blue skirt, carved, as it were, out of hundreds of layers of tulle, was rather short, and when she sat down it could be seen that she wore yellow silk breeches also embroidered at the knee with bubbles.' To billow with sex even if not seventy, it was worth giving in to Dior's wish to construct his clothes like buildings. In fact, with their padded, stiffened, double linings of taffeta and muslin, their whalebone and grosgrain waistbands, they created the perfect female shape as Dior conceived it, and were, it seemed, quite capable of standing alone. The effect, however, was oddly enough exactly the one he wished to achieve: 'flower-like' and 'ethereal', the full skirts swaying from the handspan waists made all women look fragile, whether as tall as Miss Mitford or as small as Lady Marriott who, it is said, ordered forty models each season.

It was said at the time, although he himself did not say it, that Dior's inspiration had been the costume of the peasants of his native Normandy. If this is so, the inspiration had been transmuted by his unfailing taste into pure fashion. One is chary of using the word genius as applied to dressmaking, but he was certainly nearer to being a genius than any other in that field in our time, with the possible exception of Balenciaga, who did not, however, reach his commanding position until Dior's death.

Dior's was the art that conceals art. He himself described the agonies of creating a collection from choosing the fabric (he learned from Lelong to understand the subtleties of the behaviour of materials), from sketch to *toile* to finished dress, to the actual first showing. But although always far too long, even he readily admitted that the two hours flew, for the production was stage-managed as carefully as if the salon were a theatre. The order of a Paris Haute Couture Collection was more or less ordained, beginning with day clothes and gradually working through the gamut of suits, coats to afternoon dresses, through evening dresses, short and long, and grand ball gowns to the finale – the wedding dress. Dior followed this pattern, but he always took care to alternate light and dark, and, most importantly, to punctuate this long parade with the potential best sellers so that they could not fail to catch the buyers' eyes, to place the spectacular numbers so that they provoked applause. In addition, there were the pilot models dropped in to indicate a future new line. These Dior always showed about halfway through the show. They not only indicated his thinking but woke his by that time somewhat sated audience to fresh attention. He called these numbers 'Trafalgars'.

Dior tended to give his models English names: 'Piccadilly' was a favourite, used for his first mink-lined raincoat, 'Bobby' another. After his trip to the USA he had one called 'Bronx'; none of the Americans found the courage to tell him that this was not quite the appropriate name for an exquisitely-wrought Dior dress. The name did, however, gradually disappear. As the programme, of necessity, had to be printed ahead of the actual showing, by then the order had been changed at least ten times, so that the first suit to appear was apt to be not number 1, but 14 or 27. It all added to the glorious confusion.

Dior was one of the first to christen his lines: in 1953 he produced the H line, the next year the A line. There was even a Y line. Of these alphabetical symbols, the A line was the easiest to spot, but all of them gave the press a peg on which to hang their stories.

Ginette Spanier, then directrice of Balmain's, once said of Dior, 'He can do no wrong.' Actually, he did come a cropper. In 1956, when skirts had begun to climb again, he attempted to bring them down. The photographs in retrospect are enchanting, but, alas, he was a decade too soon. By this time the influence of Balenciaga had been rising and, to a more shocking degree, that of his protégé Givenchy. In his winter collection of 1957, Dior had moved toward the unfitted line they had piloted. In October of that year he was dead at the tragically early age of fifty-five.

Perhaps, as people now say of President Kennedy, he died at the right time, for the shift he included in his final collection portended a future which might have dismayed him. As it is, he will remain a legend: a charming, unassuming man who, although shouldering the responsibilities of a vast empire, managed to embue his collections with a sense of gaiety and happiness and a lightness which only great strength can produce. Although, by the time of his death, fashion had begun to take a different course, Dior will always have two unique distinctions: with one collection he had achieved an end to which all dress designers aspire, that of, overnight, making every woman wish she were naked with a chequebook; and to him must go the credit for re-establishing Paris as a fashion centre after the long hiatus of the war.

Balenciaga

CRISTOBAL BALENCIAGA

1895–1972

Epitome of Nobility

Cristóbal Balenciaga occupies a unique position in twentieth-century fashion. It is doubtful if any talent which may emerge in the two decades left before the dawn of AD 2000, whether it be male or female, could arouse the reverence that this Spanish designer evoked from the international press, buyers, customers and the chosen few admitted to intimacy. Cecil Beaton wrote in 1954 that 'Balenciaga stands apart . . . perhaps the last of the great couturiers.' On Balenciaga's retirement in 1968, sadly remarking that the world in which the couture could flourish was finished, the *Sunday Times* headed the story 'An Epitaph to Elegance'. In 1973, a year after his death, the Metropolitan Museum of Art gave him a major exhibition organized by Diana Vreeland under the auspices of the Spanish government. The owners of the 250 items which Mrs Vreeland had collected from all points of the compass represented practically every well-dressed woman, dead or alive, while the catalogue to the exhibition contained a series of prose poems to the Master by Mrs Vreeland, Gloria Guinness and the late Baroness Pauline de Rothschild, as well as a eulogy by his parish priest. Balenciaga was, like Chanel (who was almost apotheosized after her death) and Dior, already a legend in his lifetime.

Perhaps a brief explanation is due here of why Christian Dior takes precedence over Balenciaga in this chronological series, although the latter had opened in Paris nine, ten or eleven years (the dates variously given are 1936, 1937, 1938, the last being the most likely) before Dior made his debut. It is because, despite the support of Carmel Snow, editor of America's *Harper's Bazaar* and first to perceive Balenciaga's special quality, the interruption of the war followed by the irruption of the New Look and the new talent of Dior with his gift for the publicity which Balenciaga shunned, Dior, while not exactly eclipsing Balenciaga, stole the limelight, at least as far as the press went. Balenciaga's pre-war customers were loyal. Mrs Snow chose for her much-photographed return to Paris after the war a typical soft-shouldered Balenciaga coat. Perched on her blue-rinsed white hair was one of his deliciously absurd pill-box hats, of which Pauline de Rothschild wrote 'the wit was on the head', and which he was the first to introduce.

To Cecil Beaton, Balenciaga and Dior were each 'unquestionably a genius of contemporary style'. An artist himself, Beaton saw them in terms of painters: Dior 'the Watteau of dressmaking', Balenciaga 'fashion's Picasso'. Others were reminded of music: Dior was like Mozart, a bubbling fountain of seemingly endless happy inspiration; Balenciaga like Granados 'Goyescas', sombre, brooding, dignified. In other ways the designers were opposites: Dior was essentially French, in repose wistful, with, when pleased, a shy diffident smile, cosy and unassuming; Balenciaga was as Spanish as Dior was French – dark, aquiline, proud and remote with an almost professorial austerity of expression.

The history of Balenciaga's beginnings as usual varies in detail, but there are basic similarities. Born in the fishing village of Guitaria on the Basque coast in 1895, he was the son of (take your choice) a fisherman, the skipper of a fishing fleet, the captain of a pleasure craft. (A certain upgrading can be discerned.) What is agreed is that money was scarce and his mother was a seamstress. It is doubtful if he would have remained in obscurity, but to speed his way a fairy godmother appeared: the local aristocrat, the Marquesa de Casa Torres, at whom the small boy gazed admiringly. One day, overcome by her appearance in a suit of white shantung, he could not restrain himself and exclaimed, 'How elegant'. Such a sophisticated comment by a simple peasant boy intrigued the Marquesa. She stopped and talked to him. Discovering that he could sew, she gave him a suit by Drecoll to copy. This was a tremendous challenge, a challenge to which the young Balenciagá rose triumphantly.

After this success the Marquesa continued to interest herself in him. She sent him to Paris armed with an introduction to Doucet, who, gentleman that he was, allowed him to see behind the scenes of a great couture house. Balenciaga returned home resolved to become a couturier. In due course, the Marquesa's backing enabled him to open his first shop – a tailoring shop in San Sebastian. After that, as Fanny Brice once sang, he climbed the ladder of success 'runk by runk' until the time came when he could open his own couture houses, for which he used the name Eisa, in both Madrid and Barcelona.

Wars figure largely in the destiny of couturiers as well as nations. The Spanish Civil War determined Balenciaga to leave Spain for Paris, where, with the help of Spanish friends, he took a house in the Avenue George v which eventually made that street a focus of elegance. At his first collection in 1937, the press, mostly French, were cool, if not cold – after all, he was a foreigner – but, fortunately, Mrs Snow, who never missed a chance to spot a new talent, was present. She was quick to perceive the individual flavour of his style, and although she realized that it was too new and too difficult to be warmly received at first glance, she felt it to be so compatible with her taste that she decided to be dressed by him. They became great friends, and when she wangled a trip to Paris immediately after the Liberation, she stopped off in Madrid, where Balenciaga had returned during the war, to see him.

It was for Mrs Snow that Balenciago created the collar which his close friend and protégé, Givenchy, to whom Mrs Snow introduced him, still uses – the widely-set, narrow, curled-over, back-dipping collar that became his hallmark. Mrs Snow modestly explained that it was created for her because she had no neck. Another invention was the nine-tenths sleeve for jackets and coats which adds inches to a small woman's height.

It is probably true that there is no cabal of designers who decide in which direction they will lead the public, and perhaps it is true that great designers are too proud to copy each other. Still, there are a lot of ways that the word can get round: the fabric manufacturers gossip, the workroom staff boasts, friends of the designer talk. Anyway, it is true that as soon as Dior launched the New Look his tiny waists and full skirts appeared in most major collections, soon to spread over the world. Similarly, Balenciaga's long princess evening dress flowed from a narrow top to a wide hem, dependent solely on a miracle of cut – no linings or stiffening of any kind, its movement imaginatively described by Pauline de Rothschild: '. . . the front of the long skirt running a little faster than one's walk'. This became so essential a part of every top couturier's vocabulary that it needed a highly educated eye to identify one as by the original creator.

Forgetting her early convent training, Chanel averred that she could not sew, but 'I do know,' she added, 'where to put the pins in,' and she created her clothes on live (and long-suffering) models. Balmain admitted that when he went to Molyneux he could not cut a *toile*. On his own, he, like Dior, works from sketches. ('I don't sell bits of paper,' snorted Chanel.) Balenciaga, on the other hand, cut, he tailored, he manoeuvred by hand a garment into the perfection that makes his admirers wax lyrical. 'He knows,' said Givenchy, who adopted him as a master ('One must have a *maître*'), 'how a wrist moves in a cuff.'

Chanel was always photographed during a fitting perfectly accoutred even to her hat; Dior wore a white coat rather like a hospital orderly's; Balenciaga wore a porter's smock. A prized possession of Cecil Beaton's was one of these in navy cotton given him by the master 'off his back'.

Immediately after the war, Balenciaga was showing short, full skirts, fitted bodices, with elaborately puffed sleeves or exaggerated bows. Always there were, and were to persist although gradually refined, the echoes of the traditional glittering embroideries worn by the performers at the Plaza de Toros and the dramatic flounces of the flamenco dancers. Despite the differences in the personalities of Balenciaga and Dior, there were certain, perhaps inevitable, similarities in their designs. Over the years, both showed bloused jackets, both slimmed skirts. Both showed tightly belted fitted jackets, stiffened out into a curve below the waists. Both shortened skirts, as did all Paris, Balenciaga and Givenchy, who opened on his own in 1951, doing so most emphatically.

The parting of the fashion ways between Dior and Balenciaga was slow but sure. Balenciaga had been moving increasingly away from fit. In 1952 he showed what became called the 'gentled look' – a jacket curving up in front with only a shadow of a shape, the back dropping straight and loose from the stand-away collar which he had created for Mrs Snow. Untailored suits from a master tailor frightened the press, by now brainwashed by the New Look, into silence. Mrs Snow, in her usual front row seat, rose to her feet and started to applaud. Nobody joined her. Undaunted she continued to clap, slowly and loudly. In addition she devoted the Paris issue of *Harper's Bazaar* to Balenciaga's collection. To those unacquainted with fashion magazine hierarchy, this was tantamount to instant stardom. It was also testimony to Mrs Snow's independence of judgment. The fashion world began to take heed, but the buyers were frightened into fits – they were a timid lot in those days. Balenciaga listened to them, adapted the line just enough to allay their fears, and immediately returned to what he felt and knew to be right. By 1959 his was the accepted jacket shape, so Balenciaga then indented his jacket above a sharply-projecting peplum.

In 1957, as foreshadowed in 1955, both he and Givenchy, who had moved across the street the year before, dispensed with shape entirely in dresses that narrowed gradually from drawstring necks or wide shoulders to skirts perilously near a hobble. The *Sunday Times* was the first, in September 1956, to call them, rather disparagingly, 'sacks'. The name stuck. Sacks they were and women fell into them with joy. Even Dior showed his version of these chemise dresses in his last collection before his death. In one way or another, they have been with us ever since.

In retrospect, the work of Balenciaga seems to fall into two distinct categories. One was a bold statement of fantasy. In an attempt to assess the Balenciaga and Givenchy collections of 1957, in which fantasy ran riot from Balenciaga's short black lace shift tightly-belted at the knees to Givenchy's kite-shaped sack, the *Sunday Times* (again) wrote: '... logically and inevitably over the years their ideas have reached a stage of development as revolutionary as streamlining, and not unlike it. Just as streamlining was developed for the age of speed, these clothes are for an age of science-fiction' – a fiction which became all too true and made these clothes eventually seem traditional. (The reason B. and G., as they were irreverently dubbed, are bracketed, is that in 1957 they both decided to delay their press showings until after the buyers had seen them, a delay varying from two weeks to a month after their colleagues in the Chambre Syndicale had shown; in 1965 they were to be joined by Yves Saint Laurent in an uneasy triumvirate.)

The fantasies continued – some so idiosyncratic, not to say eccentric, as to please only the aficionados. There was the double balloon evening cape of 1950 ('Look, Mummy, no hands'); the photographer's dream dress of 1952, a strapless black lace tightly tied at the waist and just below what Evelyn Waugh's black lady called the 'sit-upon', with pale silk ribbons, the skirt frilling out in tiers; the white evening dress, again strapless, of 1958, a flap to the knees in front heavily gathered under the arms, another flap falling to the floor at the back, giving the impression that the wearer was peering over a shower curtain; the flower-printed heavy silk of 1960, also strapless, with a fitted bodice in front belling out below the waist, the back cowl-drapped falling in folds to the floor, looking like nothing so much as an elegantly upholstered chair, inexplicably walking.

This is, of course, *lèse-majesté*. These experiments were the evidence of a creative imagination reaching towards a new frontier of fashion, but they were experiments rather than fashion. Along with these were other clothes whose simplicity and perfection of proportion and cut took away one's breath: the soft fall of the jackets, the set of the sleeves, the dramatic drop of a princess dress from knee-high brevity in front to trail the floor at the back, the hierarchic majesty of his jewel-encrusted shifts. These were the clothes his customers ordered again and again.

Chanel told Bettina Ballard that 'You make money on the customer who orders lots of clothes at once.' Balenciaga, on the other hand, was said to prefer the discerning customer who knew what she could wear and where she would wear it. Still, he tolerated those like Helena Rubenstein, who ordered one jewelled dress after another. One hopes he would have approved of Mrs Graham Sutherland, to whom Madame Rubenstein gave one of these priceless dresses when Graham Sutherland was painting her. Mrs Sutherland, feeling it a bit overpowering as a dress, turned it back to front, slit it down the centre and wore it as a coat. It looked wonderful. No objection was ever heard to those clients who ordered five of a favourite model so that they could be sure of having one at each of their houses, or who ordered two of each model so that they would always have one at hand while the other was being cleaned, or the one who ordered all her clothes from him down to her shorts 'because it saves so much trouble shopping around'.

Balenciaga originally became a recluse because at first he had to work so hard that he had no time to be anything else. Then it was perceived to be rather a good ploy where other designers were sometimes only too accessible. This suited his Basque temperament – austere, independent, hardworking, determined, humourless, and once decided upon a course, stubborn in its pursuit against all odds and arguments.

This reclusiveness, this pertinacious professional invisibility – he never appeared at his own showings – this aura of exclusiveness was fostered by his twin dragons, Mme Renée and Mme Véra, who denied entrance to all but the most favoured. Mme Renée once refused to allow an important buyer from one of the great American stores to bring a client, the beautiful wife of a famous film director, unless the latter brought her passport with her to prove that she was who she was. It was a little like an audience with the Pope, and the client was suitably impressed.

The anticipation started as one entered his House after admiring his small but dramatically beautiful windows, which never showed anything as vulgar as a garment, just imaginative arrangements of birds and flowers by Janine Janet (who has just decorated the new Ricci Boutique). There was never any of the excited chatter that preceded the press showings of the Dior collection, the noise and excitement accelerating as one mounted the stairs. At Balenciaga the silence was imposed by the small lift, like a padded cell, which held only four people at a time if one of them was slim. After surviving the suspicious vetting of Mesdames Renée and Véra, one was shown to one's seat where one chatted with one's neighbours in church whispers. Not for Balenciaga, as for Dior, young alluring mannequins. His were often middle-aged (like his clients), and never pretty – one exotic Oriental was for years thought to be a Chinese mandarin. They were not arrogant; they were just incredibly and unsmilingly detached. No amount of applause brought a change of expression. The collection was presented; take it or leave it. Most took it.

This serious and austere man, however, had, as was shown by his concession to the buyers, a practical side. In the chill winter of 1962 he was the first to launch warm patterned tights, suitably in his January collection. He was followed in September by Pierre Cardin, and then by so many others that by the end of 1963 journalists were calling 1962 the Year of the Leg. That same year Balenciaga also allowed boots to tramp over his hallowed carpet – not the elegant boots which came in later, but good, solid British-type Wellingtons, the kind in which all British legs had been encased that freezing year. Then there was the season in 1963 when he showed shiny plastic raincoats, the kind lesser folk could buy at the Prisunic. When a daring journalist queried this – to her – strange lapse of taste, she was severely rebuked by a buyer who said sternly that if Balenciaga showed plastic macs, that meant plastic macs had been promoted to high fashion. The fact is that it did not matter what he did as long as he did it. He had become a cult – and remains one. As Sam White wrote in the *Evening Standard* after Balenciaga's retirement, fashion Paris would 'never be quite the same without the almost brooding presence and indefinable authority of Balenciaga.' It is not.

PUCCI

EMILIO PUCCI

1914–

Renaissance Man

In his book *Minding the Store*, Stanley Marcus, writing in 1974, said that Emilio Pucci 'is the most copied designer of our time, aside from Chanel'. Mr Marcus, doyen of merchants, made his Dallas store, Neiman-Marcus, world famous, and, as its own inhabitants say, put Texas on the map. (Dallas, alas, became famous for another and tragic reason.) Mr Marcus is a man who should know, but it would have been more accurate to have said 'was' instead of 'is', for the Sixties was for both designers the decade of the sincerest flattery of imitation.

For Pucci the Sixties were the years when his vividly-printed silk shifts, signed 'Emilio' in his scratchy black italics, were in every smart wardrobe; the years when the beaches of the right resorts blazed with his beachwear (he thoughtfully provided boutiques at Capri and on the Lido for the unfortunates who may have come unprepared); the years when no female would have dared to embark on a yacht without a couple of his silk jersey dresses or go on a cruise without, at the very least, a copy; the years when his dresses technicoloured the summer thoroughfares of the more sophisticated cities. Even more than Chanel, Pucci became a status symbol and his clothes collectors' items – like signed first editions.

But although the slavish and often unworthy imitations have tailed off, Emilio Pucci is still in full strength. An unusual combination of designing talent, technical know-how and business acumen, he has parlayed these attributes across an ever widening board. In addition to his first boutiques, he now has boutiques in Paris, New York and, most recently, London. There is scarcely an area of fashion that this aristocratic Florentine has not invaded successfully. In fact, success has perched upon his banner ever since he was literally snapped into fashion on the ski slopes at Davos in 1947. There the slim elegance of his ski suit, in contrast to the Eskimo-type bundles of clothing then considered the proper wear, caught the eye of Toni Frissell, a distinguished American photographer. Her camera caught the flashing figure he (an ex-

Olympic skier) cut on the snow. Her photographs published in *Harper's Bazaar* caught the eye of the sportswear buyer for New York's Lord and Taylor, who had the outfit reproduced. Two year's later at Capri, a visiting belle caught Pucci's eye (he is known to have as sharp an eye for beautiful women as for beautiful clothes.) For her he designed some beachwear. Made up by a local dressmaker, they caught everybody's eye. Before he really knew it he was in business.

It was not quite as simple as all that. He started with printed silk squares whose originality of design (their motifs were often taken from Florentine art and architecture) and singing brilliance of colour procured him an order from Neiman-Marcus. He had made the designer's goal but it was still only a small order. That was in 1948. Six years later, in 1954, he had achieved the even more coveted Neiman-Marcus award.

It was a young fashion editor of *Vogue*, Cathy McManus (now the Marchesa di Montezemolo), who really put him on the fashion path. He mentioned to her that he had been much struck by the casual ease of the American work shirts worn outside pants. 'Why don't you,' she suggested, 'turn some of your silk squares into shirts?' These shirts with his skinny 'Capri' pants became a uniform. This was the real beginning. Pucci went on to printed dresses in silk, and later in jersey.

It was not all smooth going. There were rocks under the snow. When, in 1950, the first Italian high fashion showings were initiated in Florence, Emilio was a name; but, as a local boy, he was tucked into a corner. No corner, however, could conceal Pucci and his wares. The American buyers (all five of them at that time) spied him out – and bought. By 1955 the buyers filled the huge Sala Bianca of the Pitti Palace; in 1961 the number of buyers from all over the world had so swelled that they overflowed into corridors and, to the regret of the audience, even into the refreshment bar. The sharpest rocks were the buyers. In 1957, when he launched his jerseys, the American buyers balked. Instead of seeing the overwhelming advantage of dresses weighing only four ounces which could be tucked into a handbag and emerge uncrushed, all they saw was jersey, to them not a fashion fabric. They had been equally reactionary about his skin-tight bottom-hugging pants, which he had made even skinnier by using stretch fabric. They had failed to foresee that the craze for form-fit would wax until a shop would be opened which specialized only in pants so tight the purchasers had to lie down to get into them, while the young, following the example of Mme Recamier, would risk pneumonia by dampening their Levis so that they would cling even more closely. As so often before, Pucci was a pioneer.

The instigator and first president of the Alta Moda showings in Florence was Senor G. B. Giorgini. By 1963 Pucci had become vice – president. He had glided over the rocks. He had become a star. He was not the first to comb the globe for ideas, but he digested rather than reproduced. In his collection of 1963, inspired by a trip to Indonesia, he gave a lesson in how ethnic dress could be distilled into fashion. The sarongs, the trousered skirts, the brief embroidered net sacques, the coolie hats of Bali, Java, Borneo and Sumatra were as ideal for his resort wear as they were for his prints.

Pucci is one of nature's boutique designers, with a remarkable nose for sniffing out the seismic changes that affect fashion. He is also the most inventive and enduring talent to come out of Italy. He has survived the bickering between Florence and Rome as to which city should be the fashion capital of Italy, the squabble between the couture and the boutique (i.e. ready-to-wear) designers. In 1972 this was more or less decided for them. That year Walter Albini, who had designed five collections for Septième, decided to leave the Pitti Palace for Milan, and that year Missoni, the knitwear designer, also deserted the Sala Bianca. Others followed, with buyers and the press in their train. Pucci, however, could more than hold his own, showing his collections in the imposing ballroom of his own palace.

As Stanley Marcus has said, Pucci has 'not only made a fortune for himself but also for the countless manufacturers who copied and imitated his prints.' His thousand-year-old Palazzo Pucci in the Via dei Pucci, where after the war his family could barely heat and light a few of its many rooms, has been magnificently restored. That he was born the Marchese Emilio Pucci di Barsento is not exactly a drawback, but in the Italian Moda titles are a dime a dozen – princesses and duchesses abound; even photographers are counts. There are, in fact, so many titles that it is considered smarter not to use them. Emilio was the first to drop his. In this gallery of nobility, Pucci is one of the few whose ancestors figure in paintings by Raphael, Botticelli and Leonardo which hang in the Uffizi as well as in his own palazzo. They can be easily spotted by their astonishing resemblance to him.

Pucci was certainly the only one of the designers who came to London in 1963, for the first of the *Sunday Times* International Awards, to make his prime priority a call upon the Head of the Foreign Office. He had recently been elected the Liberal MP for Florence, a seat he occupied from 1963 to 1972. Apparently, no one had told the distinguished British official that the Liberal Party in Italy is, as an Italian friend explained, 'somewhat to the right of John Birch'. Anyway, his opinion of fashion designers took a leap up. In 1964 Pucci was elected City Councillor for Florence, a post he still holds, somehow combining it with his many other interests (for example, making wine from his own vineyards, labelled 'Chianti Emilio Pucci', sold both at home and abroad) and his designing activities. The latter are almost too many to catalogue, ranging from porcelain for Rosenthal to Ford's pride, the Lincoln Continental, and Parker pens. For his two collections a year, he designs the fabrics and prints as well as the clothes and accessories (hats, shoes and jewellery).

He is not the first dressmaker whose energies enable him to

undertake spin-offs, but his are always different. For one thing, it is said he never simply lends his name to products designed by others; and, for another, whatever new area he tackles he studies its function and then interprets it with his special flair. He was not the first dressmaker to invade the field of men's wear (Cardin did that in 1958), but in the collection in 1971 for Austin Reed in London, he added a fillip – jackets lined with his own printed silks and ties to match. He was not the first to be asked to re-design uniforms, but where most other designers have usually just simplified or elaborated existing models, Pucci, when invited in 1965 by Braniff International Airways (Dallas based), proceeded to re-think the entire problem from scratch. His task then was to dramatize the global extent of Braniff's service, which involved for its staff drastic changes in climate. According to the Braniff office in London, he did not stop at re-clothing the flight crew (male and female), but the mechanics and ground staff as well. It was, however, his wardrobe for the air hostesses that stopped people in their tracks, and presumably caused them to make for Braniff.

From the start, the clothes were daring in colour (pink, blue, lime, peach) and in exotic print motifs. His innovations were basically practical but original in execution. They included full culottes caught at the knee instead of the provocative narrow skirts, and turtleneck blouses instead of manly shirts. Practically everything was interchangeable or reversible, except the pillbox hats in Pucci prints (and even they had ear flaps that could be caught under the chin or folded away under the crown). There were clear plastic bubble helmets (astronaut-inspired) to protect both hat and hair against wind or rain, and printed Pucci boots. In 1966 he added more headline-catchers: printed leotards beneath brief shifts, bowler hats such as Peruvian peasant women wear, hooded fur coats, fur-lined boots and gloves, transparent raincoats and boots. Through the years he added and subtracted to cope with varying temperatures as new routes opened up, from shifts which could be worn alone or over full slacks in a new Pucci fabric – non-wrinkle, quick-dry nylon tricot, which he trademarked 'Emilio-jet' – to brightly coloured (emerald green and peacock blue) interchangeable outfits in light wool with crisp tailored trousers instead of leotards. Braniff having presumably made its mark, the later lines were more subdued. Pucci outfitted Braniff for twelve years. From 1977 the uniforms have been the work of Halston.

Pucci was not the first designer to create a House scent (Poiret did it in 1911) but Pucci's Vivara and Zadig have been described as sexy; so is his lingerie for Formfit and his contour-revealing 'natural' girdle. Pucci himself could be described as sexy, too. Until his marriage he, slender, dark-haired, elegant, was certainly the most eligible bachelor in the fashion world. He never made a secret of his liking for pretty girls, and the clothes he creates for them enhance rather than conceal their femininity.

Pucci's background is unusual for an Italian – and a fashion designer. He studied at the University of Georgia (USA) and took a Master's degree in Political Science at Reed College in Portland, Oregon. When he returned to Italy, he went to the University of Florence, where in 1941 he received a Ph.D. This experience seems a more suitable preparation for his subsequent career in politics than for a career in fashion, but the first-hand knowledge he acquired, as a by-product, of the extremes of climate in the USA, from the heat of the South to the snows of the Pacific Northwest, came in handy when he started to export, as did his easy command of the American idiom.

He had barely time to receive his diploma before he was caught up in the war. He became an ace pilot in the Italian Air Force, and was wounded and decorated several times. However, in 1944 his most daring exploit was to smuggle into Switzerland Edda Ciano, Mussolini's daughter, an old and dear friend then married to Count Ciano, Mussolini's Foreign Minister, whom the Nazis, no longer pally with the Fascists, had captured. He included in his cargo not only the Ciano children but the Ciano diaries as well, diaries the Germans were more than anxious to get hold of. He returned to Italy, hoping to save Ciano as well, but was caught by the Gestapo. He refused to talk even under torture and was eventually released. The war over, he resumed skiing and might be skiing still if that photographer had not spotted him.

In 1958 he married a beautiful young honey blonde from Milan, and they settled down in Florence, continuing to restore his ancestral palace. The Puccis have two children, Alessandro, twenty, studying at Buckingham College in England, and a daughter, Laudomia, a year younger.

Now, at sixty-five, Pucci is still slender, his dark hair now the man of distinction's requisite grey, and he is, it seems, more energetic than ever, flying round the world to supervise his far-flung enterprises, continuing his political and agrarian interests. As with other magic names, his success was based on timing. His vivid, unexpected colour juxtapositions and bold lively patterns came just when the post-war world, tired of khaki and mournful black, was longing for just his brand of colourful originality. The knowledge, for which he has so remarkable a flair, of production and marketing creates the solid structure on which his most novel ideas rest securely. He has reaped many honours, but his special achievement was to change the look of women under the sun.

C
AR
D
IN

PIERRE CARDIN

1922–

Magician

Pierre Cardin is less a magic name than a magician; he is certainly less a couturier than an explosion of talent of which fashion is only a part. His pale, intense face fits the magician image. It also conceals a sharp business brain, even as his philosophic pontifications veil his practical projects. He first made his name designing clothes for women, and he has adroitly used his success in his field, as his publicity rather naively puts it, to promote 'more advanced conceptions and creations' which his prestige assures will be 'perfectly commercial'. Although Cardin did not pioneer the many diversifications which are now common practice in the major couture Houses (by 1966 Dior's roof already sheltered – besides clothes and hats – shoes, stockings, girdles, gloves, scents, lipsticks...), he widened the horizons and introduced many more. In 1958 he was in the vanguard of those designing accessories for men, following an earlier foray into Charvet country by Schiaparelli and Piguet with their men's ties.

In 1961, Cardin opened his men's boutique, as had Dior and Lanvin. The Dior men's boutique was not, they said, for 'the man in the grey flannel suit', and they proved it by showing a shirt with a Cossack collar and a bib front. Lanvin's aim was toward 'specialities'. Cardin was showing high-buttoned collarless jackets, sleeveless pullovers in tweed with matching jackets, zip-fastened suede smocks instead of overcoats, pipe-stem trousers that flared at the hems, held taut by elastic ski-straps and double-breasted evening shirts. None of these sound, or indeed look, far out to today's eyes, yet they and others that were to follow started a revolution in men's clothing that was to challenge the monopoly of Savile Row, the home of British men's tailoring, whose dominance had been established by Beau Brummell 165 years before. The Cardin revolution was shorter lived than Beau Brummell's, but it opened the door to an excess of excesses.

As Cardin pared away collars and obliterated pockets, others added finery with abandon not seen, as Dr Roy Strong,

Director of the Victoria & Albert Museum remarked 'since the days of pre-French Revolutionary Europe'. The male peacock was reborn in velvet suits, fancy waistcoats (brocade or leopard skin), necklaces, bracelets, even earrings; hair was long, carefully (or carelessly) dressed; faces were a triumph of topiary work in moustaches and beards. All of this reached a crescendo in the mid-Seventies, but by 1976 there were signs that high camp was fading out. Except for the jeans set, a new sobriety was appearing. In 1979 M. Cardin himself was photographed wearing the contemporary equivalent of the Beau Brummell gospel according to Beerbohm: certain congruities of dark cloth, a rigid perfection of linen. M. Cardin, always of today, has adapted the formula. His tie, like his simply tailored suit, is white, so are his trousers; his coat, its lapels widened and sharpened, is in sober dark cloth. His now greying hair is short. He has cleverly combined yesterday's discipline with today's freedom.

He was the first to explore – and exploit – the markets of the Far East: Japan in 1958, China in 1978. In the old days before 1962, when the couture broke its own release dates, being caught sketching or, even worse, photographing at a Couture Collection meant expulsion into outer darkness. Cardin's salons were filled with exquisite Japanese in traditional dress, from whom issued faint, clicking noises. A suspicious member of the Chambre Syndical, which used to police such illicit activities, suspected them of concealing tiny cameras under their long fingernails, but she said, 'What can I do? They'll just pop them into their lacquered hair-dos.' True or false, in their kimonos and obis and led by the Japanese Ambassadress, they made an exotic contrast to the hot and tired members of the press. The journalists were hot because Cardin's salons were the most air-tight in Paris; the only time a window was known to have been opened was in 1966 at the urgent request of ex-President Nixon – a request which the late Nicole Alphand, whose husband had been Ambassador to Washington, nervously granted.

The journalists were tired because Cardin's collections were the latest in starting and the longest in Paris, exceeding in mileage even Dior's. After Cardin moved in 1970 to the vast night-club, 'Les Ambassadeurs', which he had gutted to make his 'L'Espace Cardin', the collections became an endurance test, failed, alas, by many of his most dedicated fans.

By 1976, 'L'Espace Cardin' had become a kind of miniature Centre Pompidou. Besides providing a place in which to show his collections, it houses recording studios, theatres, a cinema, a concert hall, an art gallery, restaurants. (Perhaps the last sparked his venture into food – known as 'Maxim's Line'.) He has always had an affinity with the theatre and cinema. In 1945, early in his career, he had made masks and costumes for Cocteau's film *La Belle et la Bête*. Twenty years later, in 1965, he created with Ghislaine Uhry the seductively pretty Edwardian costumes for Brigitte Bardot in *Viva Maria* whose blouses with their frill-edged high collars, long sleeves and lace trim were copied in boutiques throughout Great Britain and the USA. It is fair to assume that they started an appetite for the real thing to cater for which a rash of second-hand shops found themselves doing a land-office business. Recently he took a part in a film with Jeanne Moreau, a close friend.

As a couturier he was a cat that walked alone. This was acknowledged by the French Committee who nominated him in 1963 for one of the *Sunday Times* International Awards as 'an original designer and one of the few outside the Balenciaga orbit'. On the theory that fashion should be the result of evolution and not revolution, this was true. With Cardin there is more a sense of exploration, surprise and often excitement. His only bow to tradition is the announcement of 'lines' in his hand-outs: the Sickle Line (could that have been his pouch-back jackets?), the Mushroom Line (perhaps his pleated collars) and so on. This was odd, for his first apprenticeships had been with Paquin, Schiaparelli and Dior, who, although designers of powerful personalities, followed the formal pattern of couture presentation.

From his début on his own in 1953 in a salon in the Rue Richepanse from which the next year he was able to move to the Faubourg Saint Honoré (he now seems to own a large part of the street, as well as a grand house in the Place François Premier, and the Place Beauvau), Cardin seemed to shed all influences. One of the rare self-financed couturiers (he said in 1964 that there was no money but his own behind him) he was independent of the pressures that heavy investment imposes. In other Houses, subordinate to business interests, there was sometimes the feeling that inside every fat collection a thin designer was trying to get out his message. Cardin could follow his own bent. If he succeeded, well and good, or even better; if he failed he brought nobody else down with him. He succeeded. And dispensed with consistency.

He would introduce an idea, drop it, pick it up again. In 1957, 1958 and again in 1959 he was avowedly concerned with *'le drap'*. With an almost scientific thoroughness he investigated every permutation of cowl drapery (first introduced by Vionnet) even allowing one cowl neck to fall to the hem at the back. In 1958 he first evinced his interest in collars; round, they were gathered, tucked, pleated, sometimes doubled, always growing larger. Later that year he gave up *'le drap'* for the scissors. Cut replaced what had begun to look like a losing wrestling-match with fabric. In 1960 and 1963 he returned to the bias but in a different manner, out-Vionneting Vionnet in spiralling dresses whose virtuosity forced many a reporter to down tools. That year also saw his first use of scallops – as edging or appliqué, a pet theme he periodically brought back. Fascinated by techniques, he turned his attention to pleats – reviving sunray pleats, accordion pleats, knife pleats, cartridge pleats, all of which he put to new, as well as more usual, uses for collars, sleeves or godets. Tucking, too, obsessed him: he revived smocking and cartridge tucks.

In the restless Sixties and into the Seventies his collections were kaleidoscopic. Everything he did was the most: his collars were the vastest, his cut-outs the sexiest, his slit skirts the highest, his plunging necklines the lowest, his shifts the shiftiest, his minis the miniest, his maxis the maxiest. Fascinated by geometric shapes, he incorporated the rhomboid, the circle and the parabola into his designs. So personal and emphatic were some of his trademarks (as, for example his metallic belt buckles in curious shapes), that they were widely copied, but he always seemed to have new arrows in his quiver.

He is against yesterday, nods to today and looks to tomorrow. When the Russians shot Gagarin into space in 1961, Cardin, like Courrèges, was prepared to orbit, and in 1964 he launched his own moon strike, five years ahead of the astronauts' actual landing. Cardin was at home in the Space Age, with brief tabards over cat-suits, high leather stocking boots and space helmets. His interest in the new made him one of the first to welcome vinyl, both in entire garments or as decoration. He was also one of the first to show his men's and women's clothes on the same runway, gaining the doubtful distinction of fathering Unisex, promptly christened 'Loonisex' by *Private Eye*.

He had already begun his ready-to-wear collections: for women in 1959, for men in 1961. Clothes for children, too, were not neglected, and were first shown in 1966 according to his hand-out on 'all the available triplets in Paris'. Later, like his men's clothes, they were to have a boutique of their own. In 1979 his clothes for men and women were sold in 500 boutiques. House scents being par for the course, he added jewellery, watches and lighters. Having by then designed nearly every possible article of clothing or accessories, he turned to environment. He has designed cars and jet airplanes, he has designed radios, coffee-machines, alarm-clocks. He went into packaging: chocolates (his own make), paper tissues, record sleeves for his own LPs. He made stereophonic tape-recorders and record-players. He took a spectacular dive into house furnishings: carpets, paint, furniture (high fashion in limited editions), curtains, everything pertaining to the bedroom, the bath and the kitchen. The catalogue is enormous, including items like china, glass, puppet shows.... You name it; he does it. His licences multiply astronomically, numbering 395 in 1977, according to W, and increased by fifteen per cent in 1978 according to Cardin. Just as he was self-financed, so he insists on personally supervising everything which bears his name. His creed is that if something is called Cardin, it must have Cardin quality. As with everything except his scents which are under separate franchise, he is his own man.

In the early Seventies, although the Cardin collections were still prodigies of prodigality, more wearable clothes made their appearance among the visionary designs which had earned Cardin the reputation for making prototypes rather than clothes. This humanizing of his ascetic approach may have been due to his association with André Oliver, who joined him in 1971. Oliver is tall, handsome and as social as Cardin is retiring. Oliver must also share Cardin's creative energy for, now that the ready-to-wear has soared around the globe, Oliver designs the collections intended for France and America, still collaborates on the couture collections, and in addition has a venture of his own under his own name.

The tease is how to sum up a man who, in his early sixties, is still in top gear. Certainly, Pierre Cardin is the most original, the most individual, the most prolific of designers and with his vast empire probably one of the richest. Slight and seemingly frail, if not a magician, he must be Bionic Man.

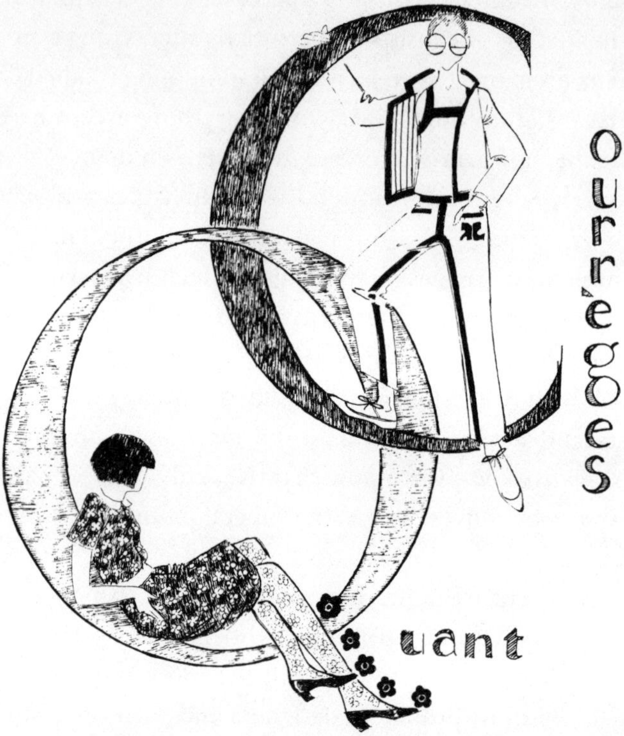
Courrèges
Quant

MARY QUANT

1934–

ANDRE COURREGES

1923–

The Sixties

Two designers epitomize the Sixties. They are England's Mary Quant and France's Courrèges. Alike in some respects, they are totally dissimilar in others. They are alike in their positive and personal approach to fashion and in their acute awareness of the world around them. They sensed the desire for physical freedom, which for both of them was expressed in the abbreviation of skirts, and by Courrèges in an emphatic belief in pants – not just for wear at home or somebody else's home, like Irène Galitzine's romantic bead-embroidered 'palazzo pyjamas' of 1962, but everywhere and round the clock as well. In almost every other way the two designers are dissimilar. Courrèges expressed order in a disordered world; Mary expressed the delight of youth in that disorder.

There are other differences as well. To begin with, Courrèges is a man and Mary Quant a woman. André Courrèges is tall and olive-skinned with shining black eyes and the taut lithe figure of an athlete, an effect he emphasized by wearing a short-sleeved white cotton shirt, white trousers and white tennis shoes reminiscent of a physical-training instructor. Mary is small, slight and brown-haired, her pointed face dominated by her large brown eyes.

Courrèges, now fifty-seven, is eleven years older than Mary, but Mary had been the first to make her mark. Courrèges was born in Pau in the Basses-Pyrenées. There pelota is as national a game as in its native neighbouring Basque country, and Courrèges became a passionate and skilful player. Although Mary's mini was dubbed a gym-slip, she is not known for an interest in games. Courrèges had wished to become a painter but was persuaded by his parents to study engineering. The strict discipline and knowledge of construction gained from this training allied with his love of sports are visible influences on his work.

Mary is Welsh, of Welsh mining-stock. Her parents, each from a small mining-village, put themselves by means of scholarships through grammar schools, on to the University of Cardiff where they both obtained Firsts and thence to London and to teaching-school. In her entry in *Who's Who*, Mary airily lists under *Educ.* 'thirteen schools, Goldsmiths' College of Art'. Although she has inherited her parents' determination, she seems more a child of her time, expressing in her clothes all of its characteristics, now clichés: the youthquake, the generation gap and, of course, the permissive society.

Mary was young enough to have been evacuated at the beginning of the last war. Courrèges was old enough to become a pilot in the French Air Force. Mary, with Alexander Plunket Greene, whom she had met at Goldsmiths' and was to marry in 1957, dove into fashion at the deep end. In 1955, together with ex-solicitor Archie McNair, who was to become a permanent member of the triumvirate, they opened the first Bazaar shop in Chelsea's King's Road, setting a pattern for the rash of boutiques that followed. Courrèges, after the war, turned to fashion design and entered the Balenciaga workrooms. There he learned from the Master to sew, cut and fit. (He still makes all his own *toiles.*) Mary has always loved to sew, but as her time at Goldsmiths' was pretty well taken up with being in love with Alexander, it is not clear what or how much she learned. However, by the time that Courrèges, after eleven years with Balenciaga, felt he was ready to realize his own ideas and set up on his own in 1961, Mary had already launched her second Bazaar shop in Knightsbridge two years before.

Mary and Alexander had opened the first shop with the intention of buying their stock in the ready-to-wear market. It was when they found none of the manufacturers seemed aware of the excitement bubbling in Chelsea that Mary decided to design and make clothes in the mood of the King's Road which she was in a perfect position to observe from Bazaar's shop window. She was so innocent that she did not know materials could be purchased wholesale, and she bought them over the expensive counter at Harrods. As the clothes sold out she would rush back for more.

The once quiet King's Road had become the beat of the Beat generation. It was patrolled by long-haired, bearded young men in leather jackets and skinny pants and longer-haired (usually uncombed) young women in duffle coats (Army surplus), tight, short skirts and black stockings or long black boots. It was not the clothes themselves that Mary wished to interpret but 'the feeling'. To her and Alexander even Teddy boys had the virtue of being 'positive', but their special love was for the dandified cinema cowboy with his high-heeled boots, skin-tight hipster pants, belts slung even lower. She was the first to absorb this look into fashion. By 1960 Mary's skirts had risen to just below the knee. They continued to rise.

It was in 1961 that Courrèges opened his first salon – small, white and throbbing with sultry Spanish guitar music. His first collections were transitional, still heavily-influenced by Balenciaga. By 1962, however, he was finding his own idiom. That year his skirts were noteworthily short. By 1963, when they had been lifted everywhere, his were the shortest in Paris. By 1964 they were shorter still. By 1968 he had reduced the skirt to a token covering over a knitted catsuit. It was the introduction of tights in 1958 that made Mary's ever-climbing skirts feasible. (By 1965 she was designing tights herself.)

To which of these designers belongs the palm for originating the mini is a teasing question. Courrèges's early dreams are not generally known, but in Mary's retrospective exhibition at the London Museum in 1975, she included three sketches dated 1958–61 of little sleeveless shifts ending just below the point of indecency and demonstrating that a straight line is the shortest distance between two points. However, photographs of these years show that her actual dresses ended at, or just below, the knee and did not reach the heights until later. The two designers were seeing thigh to thigh but it took the British with their gift for apposite abbreviation to christen instantly the abbreviated dresses 'minis', and Mary became their chief exponent. She and her mini were, as she intended, the outward and visible sign of what American journalist, John Crosby, writing in England in 1964, was to christen 'Swinging London'. Mary was swinging with it and, swinging, swept the world.

Mary and her little mini were as inseparable as Mary and her little lamb. Everywhere that Mary went the mini was sure to go, even to Buckingham Palace when she went to receive her OBE in 1966. They were an integral part of the Sixties scene. The Sixties had two faces. One was fresh and exciting: the new sound (and look) of the Beatles, the irreverence of 'Beyond the Fringe', the satiric 'That Was the Week That Was' on television, the impertinence of *Private Eye*, the garish success of Carnaby Street, the strident noise of discothèques. The other was violent and evil: the Mods and Rockers, the punch-ups of the Ton-up boys, the skinheads and the terrifying spread of drug addiction. The ripples caused by Swinging London, variously categorized as relentlessly frivolous, debauched, morally decayed or the only truly modern city, reached across the ocean. In 1965 the American *Harper's Bazaar* devoted a whole issue to it, edited by Richard Avedon. The *New Yorker* magazine published a cartoon of two mini fur-coated young things battling a snowstorm. The caption read, 'I can't think why, but winters seem to be getting colder.'

Paris was not unaffected. The not-so-fresh air of the King's Road even filtered into the scented premises of the House of Dior. In 1960, the young (twenty-five year old) Yves Saint Laurent, successor to the late Christian Dior, inhaled it and exhaled it into his Beat Collection of 1960. This collection marked two turning-points. It brought Saint Laurent's career at Dior to an abrupt end and started him off to an independent success on his own. It also signalled the fatal change of direction in fashion leadership. This now came from the streets up to the Haute Couture, where before it had come down to the street from their salons. Yé Yé fashion (its name derived from the Beatles's refrain of 'Yeah, yeah') erupted in 1964 with a whole new wave of young designers.

This was the background against which Courrèges made his private revolution. As Mary, who preceded him in 1962 into wholesale production, was putting the teenagers of the world into her uniform, Courrèges for nearly a decade put women into his. Like Mary's, his dresses were shifts, but his had cap sleeves and flared from narrow tops, their simplicity of construction outlined diagrammatically by welted seams. His coats were equally simple, their only decoration a small curved belt at the back. Where Mary did not limit herself in fabrics or colours, Courrèges preferred gaberdine, a fabric which suited his clean architectural cut. His favourite colours were those loved by Le Corbusier – palest pink, ice-blue and always white. To these he added, like a good cook, spinach-green, caramel and tomato. In pattern, where Mary was discovering (for her a jackpot) the charm of Liberty sprigged prints, his taste was for the bold and simple: window-pane checks, broad stripes.

There is little point in labouring further the similarities and dissimilarities of these two designers. Mary was for the masses by intent, aimed for a world market and scoured the world as well. As early as 1962 she could say, 'I go where the machinery is.' For her circular knit underwear ('People', she said, 'aren't flat; they're round') she went to Germany, where they weren't afraid of this new concept; for her foundations to Holland and the USA; for sportswear to South Wales; for coats to Surrey; for shoes to Bristol; for the Ginger Group to Africa and Australia. She flew so much the customs men greeted her with 'Hello, Mary.'

Courrèges was essentially couture; his accessories sprang from couture thinking: his shiny, white calf-high boots (at first open-toed, a mistake he soon rectified), his mad space-age spectacles in opaque white plastic with thin slits to see through. His most important success was with his trousers. Trousers in themselves were not new. Chanel was wearing them in the Twenties for yachting, showing them in satin for evenings at home in the

Thirties, but Courrèges's were different. They were a *tour de force* of cut, seamed for and aft for a perfect pencil-slim fit. They, with his matching flared tunic tops or briskly-tailored jackets, became epidemic among those who could afford them.

The most curious thing about Courrèges and Quant was that, in a period of worldly abandon, they were both making baby clothes: Mary for the young, Courrèges for grown-ups. Courrèges seemed to recognize this by adding in his first collection stylized baby-caps tied demurely under the chin and naive, flat-heeled shoes tied across the instep – the sort known in America as Mary Janes. The nursery image was so powerful that in London a guest surveying her hostess and two other guests of varying ages and heights all wearing the standard Courrèges dress exclaimed, 'How sweet you all look in your little pinnies.' It was, of course, a false innocence, for designers, clothes and customers were essentially sophisticated.

But Courrèges could be daring, too. In February, 1964, he showed the barest back in Paris – a white lace evening pants-suit, its top decorously covered in front, caught only at the neck at the back, opening over nothing but the golden skin of his sun-tanned model. Reversing this in his August collection of that year, he showed satin evening pants under long flowing coats, fastened at the neck and falling open in front over nothing but low-slung matching hipster pants. After this dazzling collection, the doyen of French critics announced, *'Courrèges a demodé tous les autres.'*

Stanley Marcus has written that Pucci was the most copied designer after Chanel. Courrèges was certainly another. Mary's mini length may have exposed legs round the globe, but Courrèges's crisp geometry was imitated as exactly as cheap materials permitted. These were not only cheap but often unsuitable. For example, a famous knitwear house was turning out Courrèges copies in double jersey, producing a travesty of his sharp purity of line and cut.

Troubled by this, as well as by the fact that others were profiting at his expense, Courrèges decided in 1967 to copy himself. That year he launched what he called his *'Couture Future'* – in other words, Courrèges ready-made but made by Courrèges only. He was as meticulous in the production of these as with his Couture Collection, and in his sizing, at that time the best in ready-to-wear, he exploited his engineering skills.

In 1967 a new breeze began to blow, a breeze that by 1970 had been fanned into a wind of gale force by *Women's Wear Daily*. The breeze began mildly, blowing in a gentler mood which lengthened skirts and softened fabrics. Although *Women's Wear Daily* unsuccessfully had a try at calling them *'longuettes'*, the longer length was immediately christened the 'midi'. Neither this length nor the new soft mood suited Courrèges's hard-edged style. Mary coped with both more successfully, even creating another sensation in 1970 with her hot pants – brief in length and in duration. But the tide had turned away from sensationalism, away from uniforms and uniformity, and the positive statements that characterized these two designers became diluted.

Perhaps anticipating the fitful vagaries of fashion, they were in sprinters' positions, needing no starting pistol to set them racing toward new goals. Mary was the first. Her cosmetic empire, which she had started in 1966, was already expanding to global dimensions. In 1970 she was designing household furnishings and 'domestic textiles' (whatever they are). In 1972 she had embraced bed linen, blinds and curtains. In quick succession there followed men's ties, the Daisy Doll and her wardrobe, stationery, spectacle frames and sun-glasses, ceramic mugs, hats, scarves, blouses and skirts, jewellery, handbags, children's wear, carpets, and in 1978 she got, as her publicity put it 'into beds'.

Courrèges was not quite so quick off the mark. He went into men's wear in 1973 and in 1974 opened his first separate men's boutique in Paris. He had begun with a shop within a shop at Harrods in 1968. He now has fifty boutiques – free-standing, so to speak – in Germany, Greece, Italy, Spain, the USA, Canada, Chile, Japan, Hong Kong, Australia, Saudi Arabia, the Gulf States and Lebanon, as well as two in London, one for men and one for women. His designs embrace all aspects of fashion from sportswear and sun-glasses to scarves, handbags, umbrellas and towels. He has his own scents beautifully packaged – two for women, Empreinte and Eau de Courrèges, and one for men.

Mary, as has been said, is one of a triumvirate; the other two are her genial, witty husband, Alexander Plunket Greene, whose ancestry, as aristocratic as Mary's is sturdy, gave him a disdain for convention that tunes in perfectly with Mary's; and Archie McNair, ex-lawyer and shrewd business manager. (There is a fourth but not yet working partner, Orlando Plunket Greene, born in 1970.)

Courrèges is a duo, the other member his delightful wife, Coqueline, whom he met when they were both at Balenciaga's. They became, like Mary and Alexander, inseparable from 1955, and in 1967 they married. Coqueline plays a strong supportive role in their partnership. Small and dark, in her white Courrèges from the current collection, she reminded one of those incredible tiny Russian girl gymnasts. Courrèges, his dark hair now silvered, tends to philosophize about fashion – at least in his interviews. The only light touch in a recent one with Brenda Polan of the *Guardian* was the description of what he was wearing: '. . . a pale pink cotton shirt tucked into pale pink cotton trousers tucked into white boots.'

Mary and Alexander take their work seriously, but they laugh at themselves. They roared when the head of the Paris bureau of *Women's Wear Daily* told them he had told Chanel that Mary had said she was one of the greatest designers who had ever lived, to which Mademoiselle replied, 'Coming from Mary Quant, that is a very small compliment indeed.'

If Mary and Courrèges are no longer the *Wunderkinder* of fashion, they are alive and well and in big business – and laughing all the way to the bank.

Harpers BAZAAR
VOGUE
CARMEL SNOW
Edna Woolman Chase

VOGUE

EDNA WOOL[redacted]SE

1877–1[redacted]

CARM[redacted]

1887–[redacted]

Harper's [redacted]

A Magazine [redacted] an [redacted]

The magazine is American *Vogue*. The editor is Carmel Snow. Mrs Snow, after eleven years on *Vogue*, had left to become editor of *Vogue*'s greatest rival, *Harper's Bazaar*.

The atmosphere engendered by the two publications was reminiscent of a prize fight. At either end of the ring were the promoters: *Vogue*'s publisher, Condé Nast, and *Harper's Bazaar*'s William Randolph Hearst. The protagonists were the editors: for *Vogue*, Quaker Edna Woolman Chase; for *Harper's Bazaar*, Irish Carmel Snow – powerful and resourceful fighters behind their fragile, feminine exteriors, with sharp brains under their delicately blue-rinsed white hair.

Condé Nast, St Louis born, urbane New Yorker by adoption, had purchased in 1909 a dainty woman's weekly, its little finger well out, and with it acquired two priceless assets – its magic name and the young Edna Woolman Chase, who had joined the magazine in 1895, starting in the circulation department addressing envelopes. That same year, another publisher had come out of the West to conquer New York, but William Randolph Hearst was no young Lochinvar. Although each of these men was a brilliant and ambitious publisher, Nast concealed his shrewd commercial aptitude behind a suave façade. Hearst, on the other hand, soon gained the reputation he was to carry to his grave, that of a rabble-rousing buccaneer, chief proponent of the gutter press. In 1913 he, too, purchased a modest little weekly called *Harper's Bazar*. Mr Hearst added an 'a' but changed little else until 1932 when he lured Carmel Snow from *Vogue* to *Harper's Bazaar*. This was an event which caused almost as much of a furore as Diana Vreeland's decision thirty years later to move in the opposite direction. Mrs Snow had been considered Mrs Chase's heir apparent, and Mrs Chase took the defection hard, Mr Nast even harder. He never again spoke to Mrs Snow from the day she left until his death in 1942. Mrs Snow was more generous and paid him full tribute for all that she had learned under his banner. Although she was accused of disloyalty, Mrs Snow's decision, in retrospect, made sense. She would have had to hang about for her throne almost as long as Edward VII had for his, for Mrs Chase did not in fact relinquish the reins until 1952. (She died in 1957, the year Mrs Snow retired.)

Now that a bitter personal element had entered into what had been a purely business competition, the battle between the two publications was joined. An onlooker might have thought the contest unequal. In 1929 Mrs Chase became not only editor-in-chief of American *Vogue* but also of British *Vogue*, founded in 1916, French *Vogue*, founded in 1921, as well as a short-lived German *Vogue*. As Condé Nast's publishing enterprises expanded, Mrs Chase had immense resources at her disposal.

After the First World War Mr Nast purchased *La Gazette du Bon Ton*; he also purchased its incomparable editor, Lucien Vogel. In 1912 M. Vogel had assembled a stable of the most elegant and finely-bred racehorses – young men-about-town, their self-conscious dandyism inspired by their idea of Beau Brummell. They also happened to be gifted artists as well. M. Vogel gave them a delectable showcase – the most elegant small fashion publication imaginable. It is known that Vogel was a catalyst. He must also have been a strong influence, for, once gathered together, the artists (although each preserved his own identity) had a kind of house style which made their work immediately identifiable with the *Gazette*. Aesthetic considerations aside, the solid worth of the purchase was that the *Vogues* had access to the adorable pens of artists like Boutet de Monvel, Georges Barbier, A. F. Marty, Charles Martin, Georges Lepape, Paul Iribe. As the *Gazette* carried on until 1925, other artists were added to the founder members: Dufy, Drian, Brunelleschi, and Benda. To *Vogue* in the Thirties and Forties, again via Paris, came Christian Bérard, Vertès, Dali, Eugène Berman, Raoul Bouet-Willaumez, René Bouché. All of these enriched *Vogue*'s pages and covers. Mrs Chase, who loved the story-telling charm of the Bon Ton boys, strongly disapproved of opium-smoking Bérard and of his highly sophisticated style. She held on to him because, according to Mrs Ballard, she knew that if she let go, *Harper's Bazaar* would snap him up. When she did, they did. *Vogue* eventually got him back, but not before *Harper's Bazaar* had snaffled photographer Hoyningen-Huene.

It was a rough game of tit-for-tat, and there was a constant to-ing and fro-ing between the magazines; but two artists were faithful to *Vogue*: Cecil Beaton, who had made his debut as a sketcher in 1928, and Eric, as Wisconsin-born Carl August Erickson signed his work. Beaton developed through many phases into the masterful photographer he is today. Eric developed a narrative style of fashion reporting, quite different from that of the Bon Ton beaux, drawing the clothes on models in the currently fashionable stance in the currently fashionable places where it was assumed the clothes would be worn. His drawings were elegant and snobbish – but so was *Vogue*.

Vogue was rich in photographers too: Baron de Meyer, Beaton, besides the faithless Hoyningen-Huene (another Baron), Horst B. Horst, Erwin Blumenfeld, Irving Penn . . . but for fifteen years (from 1923 to 1938) their greatest star was Edward Steichen. They also rejoiced in one of the greatest art directors, the sole – and most valuable – legacy from *Vogue*'s abortive foray into Germany in the late Twenties: Mehemed Fehmy Agha (always referred to as Dr Agha), a Ukrainian born of Turkish parents. Dr Agha succeeded in opening out the pages of *Vogue*, freeing the photographs from their neat box frames, introducing contemporary typography and, what was harder, white space. To Mrs Chase white spaces was waste space. But Dr Agha won.

It was with this formidable array of talent, called by Mrs Snow 'the best tools in the world', that she had to compete. In addition, instead of useful, flourishing off-shoots, Mrs Snow had only one – British *Harper's Bazaar*, which had been launched in 1929. There was an office in Paris but it was small and only seemed to go into overdrive when she arrived; but she did have the support (although she scarcely reached Mrs Snow's shoulder) of Marie-Louise Bousquet, a wicked, witty monkey of a woman of unconquerable gaiety and gallantry, who became her Paris editor in 1938. She knew *tout Paris*, and they crowded into her tiny salon on her famous Thursday afternoons. Although eventually crippled by arthritis, Madame Bousquet never missed a fashion opening, arriving with Mrs Snow in her Mini car which she drove the way Frenchmen cross the Place de la Concorde, as described by Nancy Mitford in *The Blessing*: '... chatting away, looking neither to right nor to left ...' Both women were compulsively generous. As the phrase goes, they would give the clothes off their backs, and often did.

Mrs Snow also had to leave behind her the luxurious *Vogue* offices, designed to impress visitors, awe manufacturers and demonstrate *Vogue*'s taste – and, incidentally, its prosperity – for premises she described as 'looking like a small-town newspaper office'. Indeed, when Ray Milland, star of the film *Lady in the Dark*, which was based on *Harper's Bazaar*, came to see the reality, he asked, surveying the dingy surroundings, where the offices were. The techniques of putting together a magazine was equally primitive and the staffing rather shaky. Fortunately, Mrs Snow's assistant at *Vogue*, Frances McFadden, had followed her to *Harper's Bazaar*.

Mrs Snow had started as fashion editor. The editor, Arthur Samuels, was really a literary editor and a good one. He had, to his credit, Anita Loos, whose *Gentlemen Prefer Blondes* had given the magazine a boost, Dorothy Parker, both Waughs, Evelyn and Alec. He was not interested in fashion or the look of the magazine, and spent his time locked in his office reading. This was just as well, for Mrs Snow's new broom was sweeping up a cloud of dust. Her coups filled the air – like confetti at a wedding.

Her first was to capture the super-smart Mrs Reginald Fellowes as Paris editor. Her next was to discover Hungarian photographer Martin Munkacsi who took for her the first action (as opposed to studio) fashion photographs. That it was a cold November day, that the model in only a bathing-suit and light cape was frozen stiff, was unimportant. The photograph of a girl running along the beach with her cape billowing in the wind was like the wind of change that was blowing through *Harper's Bazaar*. Mrs Snow's next coup was to capture in 1934 the other great art director, Alexey Brodovitch, a match for *Vogue*'s Dr Agha. To *Harper's Bazaar* he brought a look of vitality, excitement and a new concept of layout. That year Mrs Snow was made Editor, Arthur Samuels resigned, and a literary editor, Beatrice Kaufman, was appointed. This proved to be another of Mrs Snow's astute appointments, for first under Mrs Kaufman and then her successor, Mary Louise Aswell, *Harper's Bazaar* continued to publish budding talent which happily bloomed: Jean Stafford, Eudora Welty, Carson McCullers, Rebecca West, Anne Lindbergh, Dylan Thomas, e. e. Cummings, Kenneth Tynan.

When Mrs Fellowes resigned, Mrs Snow pulled off still another inspired coup. She caught Diana Vreeland in her net. This was the beginning of a troika that made fashion magazine history: Snow, Brodovitch and Vreeland – three pairs of eyes instantly recognizing new talent and each knowing how to exploit it to its best advantage. Mrs Snow was conquering Paris. Brodovitch perceived the quality of Louise Dahl-Wolfe, who was to become one of the most skilful and subtle colour photographers. He was also filching more truants from *Vogue* (or was it vice versa): anyway, Dali, Tchelitchew and Dufy began to appear on *Harper's Bazaar*'s covers and pages as well as *Vogue*'s. They were augmented by other artists: Marc Chagall, Felix Topolski, Isamu Noguchi, Ben Shahn. Brodovitch also introduced Picasso, Matisse, Braque, Brancusi, Giacometti and Jackson Pollock into the magazine. And, of course, it was Brodovitch who spotted Richard Avedon, certainly one of the most distinguished photographers ever to train his lens on fashion. (He was to leave *Harper's Bazaar* to follow Diana Vreeland when she went to *Vogue*.) Mrs Vreeland was, as she would have said, attending to her knitting

– initiating and projecting fashion – and inspiring copy. It was a wonderful team – full of life, gaiety, individual eccentricities and dizzily high standards, its captain Mrs Snow.

Of course, both Mrs Snow and Mrs Chase made their mistakes. Mrs Snow's was to get rid of Erté because he had been doing covers for *Harper's Bazaar*, in her opinion, for far too long. Mrs Chase's mistake – or was it Condé Nast's – was to fire Dorothy Todd, one of the early editors of British *Vogue*. Mrs Chase admitted her virtues: Miss Todd was an intellectual deep in Bloomsbury 'with a gift amounting to genius for spotting winners': first to introduce Cocteau's drawings to England, to publish Gertrude Stein, to show the work of Le Corbusier. The roster of her then young contributors is still imposing: Raymond Mortimer, Peter Quennell, David Garnett, the Sitwells, Aldous Huxley .... Madge Garland, who was there, says that there never was another magazine where one could see what was new in every facet of art everywhere – England, France, Italy. *Vogue*'s cosy features on shopping, home and beauty left Miss Todd cold. Miss Todd's *Vogue* was not a commercial success, and she had to go. It is perhaps asking too much that Mrs Snow, with all her flair and intuition, should have foreseen in 1932 that in 1965 those very Erté covers she had so disliked would become collectors' items, or that Mrs Chase, a sound editor and brilliant administrator, could have known in the early Twenties that the Bloomsburys would become a rage in the late Sixties and early Seventies.

Mrs Chase's arrivals in London were, like Elizabeth Arden's, in the nature of state visits with everything laid on, from royal Ascot to royal weddings and funerals. It is not clear that she ever visited Buckingham Palace itself, as did Miss Arden, but the latter's entrée was due more to her interest in horses than to the power of her cosmetic empire. However, a survivor of those days recalls that Condé Nast did get to the Palace, her memory sharpened by the fuss about getting him some knee-breeches.

Paris was the scene of Mrs Snow's triumphs where she was, as Bettina Ballard wrote, 'the single, most powerful figure ... her small, thin frame dwarfing the rest of the fashion press with an authority that seemed to bristle from her bones.' No collection ever began until she arrived, impeccably dressed, her short, fluffy hair topped by a Balanciaga pillbox. Although she retired in 1957, she continued to attend the Paris collections twice a year. As Mary Louise Aswell wrote, 'She was still editing her magazine. For nobody. For no one. Except herself.'

In 1959, two years after Mrs Chase's death, the Condé Nast interests passed into the hands of newspaper tycoon Samuel I. Newhouse and his wife, Mitzi. The story goes that Mr Newhouse had asked his wife what she wanted for a wedding anniversary. When she replied that she would quite like *Vogue*, presumably meaning a subscription, he bought the lot. The *Vogue*s have continued to multiply: *Vogue* Australia, 1959; *Vogue* Italia, 1965; *Vogue* Brazil, 1975; German *Vogue* (revived) 1979. The flagship of the fleet is British *Vogue*, edited since 1964 by Beatrix Miller, who had been one of the triumvirate that produced the *Queen* magazine. British *Harper's Bazaar* amalgamated with *Queen* in 1970 and, under the editorship of Willie Landels, who had been *Queen*'s art director, it flourishes. American *Harper's Bazaar* continues, edited by Anthony Mazzola, ex-*Town & Country*.

But the two pioneering editors are the ones best remembered. Both Mrs Chase and Mrs Snow were dedicated women, and their appearance of fragility belied their capacity for hard work. Mrs Chase had strict principles and a certain rigidity, stemming perhaps from her Quaker background; Mrs Snow had a high-flying, adventuresome spirit backed by her strong religious faith which derived from her Irish Catholic origin. It is not unnatural that, working as they did on the glossiest magazines, both were socially ambitious. Each married well, Mrs Chase had one daughter, Ilka, with whose collaboration she wrote her autobiography; Mrs Snow had three. Mrs Chase, though not pretty, cultivated a Greuze-like daintiness and a grande dame manner, the kind that makes a young person feel that she must have used the wrong fork. Mrs Snow, with her tip-tilted nose and wide smile, never needed to stress her dignity and seemed as young as the young people she delighted in. Both shared the same goal – to lift the level of taste – but where Mrs Chase was restricted by her sense of convention, Mrs Snow was always ready to take a chance. As she said to her niece, Nancy White, three months after Miss White had succeeded her as editor, 'Where's the surprise?' They were two remarkable editors, but the difference is that Edna Chase was *Vogue*'s creation, while *Harper's Bazaar* was Carmel's.

W
JF
JOHN FAIRCHILD

W and JOHN FAIRCHILD

1927–

A Newspaper and a Publisher

The newspaper is *W*; the publisher, John Fairchild. Both are American. *W* is the offspring (born in 1971) of *Women's Wear Daily*, a tabloid-sized trade paper started in 1902. John Fairchild is the grandson of the founder. *WWD*, as the parent paper is known to those concerned with fashion, is so solid in its content, so authoritative in its information that it has been called the Bible of the rag trade. This at the time was intended as a compliment. It is still a Bible, but the rag trade along with cloak and suit (American) and mantle manufacturers (British), with their pejorative connotations of cheapness, immigrant labour and distant echoes of sweatshops, have become extinct terms. As Mollie Parnis, American ready-to-wear designer, is quoted as saying, the trade has now become 'the fashion business' – a distinction with a difference. This upgrading has been in great part due to John Fairchild, tall, dimpled-chinned, product of Kent School and Princeton. When he joined *WWD*, it was heavy on facts, light on readability, stodgy in appearance – in fact, typographically illiterate.

In 1955 (the date has also been given as 1954) Mr Fairchild became head of the *WWD* Paris bureau. In the years he spent there, he became fascinated by the outsize personalities of the couturiers (and couturières) and the gossip that kept their world in a constant state of ferment. All were involuted: the personalities jealous and temperamental, the politics often as deadly as gang warfare, the gossip titillating, scandalous and only rarely true.

Chanel, who had just made her come-back, was the greatest in-fighter of them all. Her addiction to feuding seemed to attract rather than repel Mr Fairchild. It certainly kept things on the boil, provided entertainment and, above all, good copy. John Fairchild appeared to be enthralled by Chanel's monumental egotism and her ill-concealed contempt for the press. He became one of the few journalists to be admitted to her friendship. (The late Bettina Ballard, who had known her before the war, had been another.) The heights were reached literally and figuratively when in due course he was granted the much sought-after privilege of perching space on the steps of the winding staircase in her salon, at the top of which Chanel herself always sat.

At the end of five years (or was it six?), in 1960, Mr Fairchild returned to New York. Along with his luggage and family, he brought back with him a head full of ideas. He instituted a gossip column, 'Eye', in which could be retailed spicy titbits about fashion and the fashionable. If *WWD* was required reading for all concerned with the fashion trade, 'Eye' quickly became as compulsory for those whom that industry was dedicated to serve. *WWD* was soon acquiring a society readership similar to that in England who read Jennifer, in America are devotees of Eugenia Sheppard (who started her career on *WWD* and returned briefly after the demise of the *New York Herald Tribune* in 1966) and Suzy Knickerbocker. It was Miss Sheppard, when she was writing her 'Inside Fashion' column for the *New York Herald Tribune*, who first enlivened her fashion reports by interlarding them with society gossip. In 'Eye', Mr Fairchild adapted her formula to his particular brand of 'Have you stopped beating your wife' journalism. 'Eye' printed rumours, often invented, often malicious, and then retracted them several weeks later when readers would have forgotten just what the rumours were that were 'squashed' or what was being 'denied'. The damage, of course, had been done. This tactic made 'Eye' quite different from the other gossip columns, which eschew destructive items and appeal mainly to those who like to see their names in print and to those who wish they were. In 1970 *Times* magazine called him '. . . the most feared and disliked man in the fashion-publishing field'.

The 'Eye' courted Society. Its spies lunched at the fashionable restaurants Mr Fairchild referred to as 'muncheries' and reported the presence of their favourite socialites, journalists and designers. *WWD* photographers were posted outside the doors and inside as well. The photographs of the favourites were as flattering as candid shots can be, but those out of favour were somehow always caught with their mouths full, looking like chipmunks storing nuts in their cheeks against the coming winter. The restaurants were called by code names, familiar to *WWD*'s readers – X for La Grenouille (sometimes also called the Frog Pond), Y for Caravelle or the latest smartest eating-place, Z for La Côte Basque – who flocked to them to be seen or to see. The latter were bundled into dim backroom recesses, referred to by *WWD* as the 'Catchup Room' (at the Grenouille), by others as 'Siberia'. To be noted by a *WWD* eagle 'Eye' reporter being escorted there was social death. In the smart enclaves of the restaurants everybody was so busy waving at each other, perhaps in an attempt to catch the 'Eye', that Polly Devlin, reporting for the *Evening Standard* from New York, wrote that they all looked as if they were drowning and signalling for help.

In 1967 Diana Vreeland was quoted as saying: 'I think the only thing people are interested in is people . . .' In 1969 Mr Fairchild was quoted as saying: 'What's interesting about fashion is not the clothes, but the people wearing them.' Mr Fairchild is supported in this theory by the American appetite for cult figures and has profited by it. In the Sixties an unknown young matron, Mrs Leonard Holzer, was made, as Baby Jane Holzer, into a 'celebrity' by the joint efforts of John Fairchild and Diana Vreeland, then on *Vogue*. As First Lady, Mrs Kennedy was called by *WWD* 'Her Elegance' and photographed and written about constantly. She has now been demoted to 'Jackie O' but equally featured. The late Mrs William Paley, referred to by her nickname of Babe, and Mrs Loel Guinness, 'The Ultimate' to *WWD*, were other goddesses. Gloria Guinness reciprocated by including Mr Fairchild's photograph, along with those of Prince Philip, General de Gaulle and Mr and Mrs Paley to illustrate an article she wrote for *Harper's Bazaar* on 'Who's Chic, Who's With It'. Mr Fairchild cultivated the Beautiful People (and is credited for thus naming them). Affecting to despise them, he still used them to decorate his pages and fill the 'Eye'. Only English titles seem to confuse him or his editors. The wife of a knight will be called Lady Mary Smith, thus making her the daughter of at least an earl. The same treatment is given to the wife of a peer. But nobody minds a bit of elevation. Except perhaps the British reader.

For the rest of the paper, Mr Fairchild demanded scoops and got them by fair means or not so fair. Realizing that even a specialist paper could not ignore the effect of politics and politicians upon the industry it depended upon, he introduced political features. He sought out superb fashion illustrators like Kenneth Paul Block for eye-catching front-page drawings. One feature he did not touch, and one that before 'Eye' only the fashion business was aware of, was the theatre section. If it seemed inscrutable that a paper devoted to facts and figures within a clearly defined parameter should make space for the reviews of plays, the answer is simple. The New York theatre is nourished and to a degree supported by the clothing manufacturers, who, seeing it as an easy and acceptable means of entertaining out-of-town buyers, book blocks of seats for this purpose. This gives the *WWD* theatre critic almost as much influence in his field as the rest of *WWD* has in its.

In every other way John Fairchild had by 1965 transformed the paper. From back seats at collections, its reporters moved to the front row. He had become a power before whom designers and manufacturers, like sweet Alice, wept with delight at his smile and trembled with fear at his frown. He had also been made Vice-President and Publishing Director of Fairchild Publications, and in addition he had found time to write a book, *The Fashionable Savages*, in which he lashed out impartially at American fashion, stores and manufacturers (whom he divided into categories: Creators, Realists and Giants – he is a great one for coining epithets). In 1967 Fairchild became President, and celebrated by writing an anti-Beautiful people book, *The Mayflower Couple*.

After his return to New York he continued to cover the Paris Collections. There he consolidated his position with Chanel and became infected by the virulent germ of her feuding. For it, he utilized his 'Eye' technique to its fullest. When, in 1960, Yves Saint Laurent was booted into the army to be replaced by Marc Bohan, Fairchild espoused the Saint Laurent cause – a course which, as it turned out, showed admirable foresight. His partiality showed most clearly after Saint Laurent opened on his own in 1962, when at the first opening and all the subsequent ones the entire staff of the Paris office of *WWD*, plus Mr Fairchild himself, sat in the front row applauding each model. If his partisanship had been limited to that, it would just have been a display of loyalty and support.

However, this was not enough. In the pursuit of his vendetta against the House of Dior, his victim became the innocent Marc Bohan. The hounding of this unfortunate designer took the form of venomous little items in 'Eye': it recorded that Bohan's collections were flops, that buyers were few at the buyers' showings and that readers who might have intended to go should save their caution money. None of these allegations were borne out by the facts, as shown by a check of attendance at the buyers' showings and of the fabric manufacturers who know the score on re-orders of material. While it lasted, it was merciless, but eventually a concordat was reached. Paris buzzed with rumours on how this had been achieved, but the parties concerned remained silent.

The London *Sunday Times* had defended Bohan. *WWD* responded by starting a feud with this paper, first attempting with the help of Chanel to prevent its first International Fashion Awards of 1963 from taking place and then afterwards, when it did despite their efforts, giving the showing of the winners a blasting review. The sniping lasted for two years and then stopped as suddenly as it had begun.

In 1968, a year after John Fairchild had succeeded to the presidency of all the Fairchild Publications upon his father's retirement, he negotiated a profitable merger with Capital Cities Broadcasting Corporation, becoming one of its executive Vice-Presidents. He remains Chairman of the Board of *WWD*. As one of his staff says, 'John still calls the turns.' The most important 'turn' came when he perceived that *WWD* was acquiring a new readership through 'Eye', a readership not interested in purely trade information. In 1972 he hived off 'Eye' and the latest fashion news, heavily illustrated, into *W*.

Where *WWD* is a fat little tabloid, *W* is slimmer and newspaper size. It is printed on heavy paper permitting even better colour reproduction. Mr Fairchild was one of the first to appreciate that today people realize that clothes are only one part of fashion. Fashion is the way they live, where they play, what they eat and how they serve it, as well as what they wear. Both he and 'Eye' have mellowed. 'Eye' is still there (much less waspish), but pride of place is often given to 'They Told W' – a feature consisting of postage-stamp-size photographs of personalities and their replies to pertinent (and sometimes impertinent) questions. Parties are covered in depth instead of paragraphs – and liberally illustrated. Political figures and successful (no failures allowed) professional people are given full-scale interviews. Powerful people are featured as often as Beautiful ones.

A distinctive accomplishment of *W* is the freshness with which it approaches hackneyed subjects. Even beauty features are made lively. A typical issue with the emphasis on beauty exemplifies the ingenuity with which it is handled. The front page head-lined 'Beauty: Facing Change' relieves the tedium of hair-styles by combining them with a selection of the Beautiful People (Jackie O., Princess Caroline of Monaco, Gloria Vanderbilt) as they looked in 1979 with sketches of how they could look in 1980. This juxtaposition follows Mrs Vreeland's dictum that 'the only thing people are interested in is people'. Within this section (the whole of *W*'s 54–64 pages are sectionalized) and between an impressive array of advertisements, many full-page, are stories on parties in New York and a spread of one in Washington, each heavily-garnished with photographs of the guests. 'Eye' covers a Washington party from another angle; the back page is given over to 'They Told W' on a variety of subjects.

Section two is devoted to the pleasures of Normandy, brought into the *W* ambit by an introduction beginning 'Prince Charles plays polo here, Guy and Marie-Hélène de Rothschild raise studs here, Gloria Guinness has an airstrip here . . .' and concluding with, 'If there is one French province that attracts international élitism, it's Normandy. Today's Norman residents are just as illustrious and grandiose as the feudal dukes who controlled the river Seine from their hilltop fortresses.' This is pure *W*: snob value names and a bit of spoon-fed history. The feature ends with a page on 'Norman Cuisine' with mouthwatering photographs and a recipe for 'Tarte Normande Flambée' thrown in.

Section three is a hold-all. It leads with a bow to films and the theatre: a feature on Hollywood's Richard Gere and one on the producer-writer husband-and-wife team, George W. George and Judith Ross. These are followed by 'The Ultimate', a profile of a Japanese restaurant in Tokyo; and a spread on the late Katherine Cornell's house in Vineyard Haven, Massachusetts (*W* loves the Island and Island residents). The section ends with a full page devoted to British naturalist, Gerald Durrell.

Sections four and five are given over to 'Eating In', with photographs of the dining-tables of In people who eat in, photographic close-ups of the food as they serve it and some of their favourite recipes.

Section six picks up the beauty lead, this time make-up, with amusing sketches.

Section seven returns to hair, backed up with four pages of photographs of well-known ladies and their replies to 'What They Want' as beauty aids in the future.

This adds up to something for everybody – and all of it done with dash and characteristically *W* style.

(It is only fair to say that what with the heavy paper and the unstapled sections folded separately, *W* tends to have a life of its own. The sections slip merrily to the floor, and, according to the depravity of inanimate objects, usually out of sequence, which a lack of index doesn't exactly help. This may be no inconvenience to the reader, but it certainly makes the task of the earnest researcher that much harder.)

The beauty issue was chosen because of the verve and skill with which a hackneyed – and usually dull – subject was handled, but other issues, also picked at random, contain items which show Mr Fairchild's breadth of interests. These, unexpected and often startling, add a zest like the twist of lemon in a martini. For example an issue on '... The Best in Fashion' follows two pages on Saint Laurent with an article on cancer by experts. An issue traditionally devoted to the Paris Couture collections, and headlined with, for *W*, an unusually bad pun, 'Paris has a fit', (more typical is one on the Fireplace: 'An Old Flame Revisited'). The issue also contains a two-page interview with US National Security Adviser Zbigniew Brezinski, looking remarkably relaxed amid the extravagances of high French fashion. Another issue featuring 'Easy American Fashion' surprisingly includes an interview with art collector Armand Hammer. None of these men are reputed to concede interviews easily. That they do so for *W* is an indication of the clout wielded by the paper and its publisher. In the heyday of *Life* magazine, one of their top photographers, indulging in the kind of grouse endemic to that profession, was asked why he didn't leave. His answer was simple: 'If I want a story, all I have to do is knock on the door and say I'm from *Life* – and the door opens.' Today this is clearly as true with *W*.

Mr Fairchild, now fifty-three and despite his greying hair retaining his youthful Ivy League image, must be well satisfied, for *W* is now the tail that wags the *WWD* dog. The circulation figures in late 1979 show *WWD* at 70,000 (95% in the USA, 3% in Canada, 2% in the rest of the world) – a drop from the 85,000 quoted in 1970. But that may be attributed Mr Fairchild's disastrous attempt that year to play Canute against the fashion tide by promoting the midi with a carrot-and-stick technique – the carrot of good publicity in *WWD*, the stick of bad. The infant *W* has saved the situation. It has already reached a circulation of over 200,000 (95% at home, 5% abroad). An Italian edition of *W* is in the works. A Japanese edition of *WWD* was launched in April 1979.

John Fairchild's early yellow journalistic style has turned to blue blood. He is no longer the sharpest needler in the needle trade. *W* is now a considerable rival of the glossy magazines, and Mr Fairchild has proved himself a publisher with a steady finger on the pulse of the times, his telescope to his good eye.

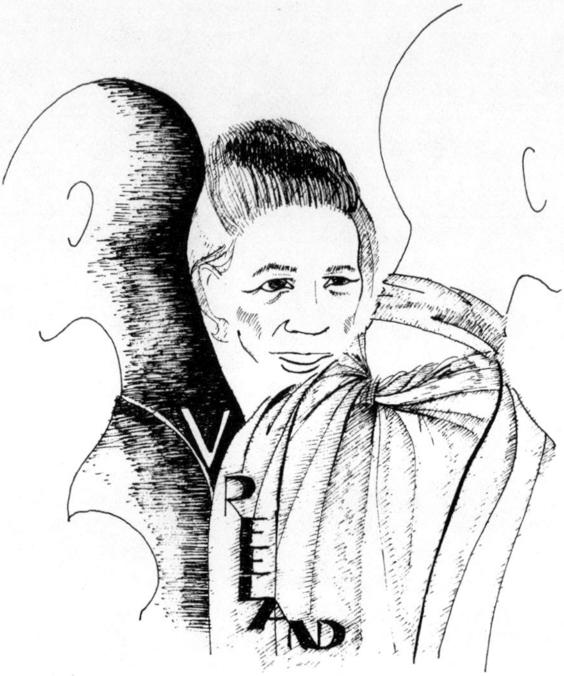
VREELAND

DIANA VREELAND

190?–

Fashion Ultimate

It may seem strange that one of the most potent names in fashion today belongs to a woman who did not start her career until she was thirty and then with a part-time job on *Harper's Bazaar*; who did not achieve editorship until her late fifties when after twenty-seven years she left the *Bazaar* in 1962 to edit American *Vogue*; who was in her late sixties when ten years later she was fired from *Vogue* and moved to the Metropolitan Museum of Art, where as Special Consultant she transformed its Costume Institute. During these years, Diana Vreeland has played three parts: a leading lady on *Harper's Bazaar*, a star on *Vogue* and a Super Star at the Met. She has been the most written about and quoted fashion personality of the post-Second World War years, if one excepts the ponderous or fulsome biographies of dress designers of the past or the more light-hearted ego-trips politely designated as 'autobiographies' by contemporary designers themselves. It is said that Mrs Vreeland has refused to be tempted to join the ranks of the latter, even for what are rumoured to be astronomical sums.

Her fame began from a low profile, partly because she was, at the beginning, one of a dedicated, gifted and adventurous team. At *Harper's Bazaar* there was editor Carmel Snow, who discovered Mrs Vreeland, art editor Alexey Brodovitch, who discovered Richard Avedon, and literary editor Beatrice Kaufman, who discovered the Southern school of writers headed by Truman Capote. Surrounded but not overwhelmed by these talents Mrs Vreeland discovered herself.

It was also partly because, during her long years at *Harper's Bazaar* (variously given by her as twenty-five, twenty-seven and twenty-eight), she could only be induced to cover the Paris collections once. It was shortly after the war, and her reaction to the overheated salons and the overheated journalistic rivalries was typical: 'It's all too sordid.' Equally, she avoided Seventh Avenue, the hub of the New York ready-to-wear industry, except for a few designers who had for her a special significance. She did not ignore

Paris, but she went independently to order her own clothes. Nor did she ignore the manufacturers themselves, whom she both puzzled and stimulated. They were puzzled by her vocabulary – 'pzazz', a word coined by the Harvard Lampoon boys, as Mrs Snow called them, who were writing copy for a special issue of the magazine. This word Mrs Vreeland made so much her own that many think she invented it. They were puzzled by her pronunciations – 'corduroi' for corduroy, 'slayzy' for sleazy, and 'Chelanāzy' for Celanese, an artificial fabric she found 'slayzy'. They were stimulated by her ideas which could be summarized in her advice to a junior editor: '... never fear being vulgar, just boring, middle-class or dull.' Mrs Vreeland's suggestions were sometimes shocking, always inventive, often not commercial, but they were never 'boring, middle-class or dull'.

She joined *Harper's Bazaar* shortly before the Second World War, lured by Mrs Snow, who wanted a successor to Mrs Reginald Fellowes. In the socially-impeccable Mrs Vreeland, Mrs Snow found the perfect answer. Starting on a part-time basis, Mrs Vreeland was soon promoted to fashion editor, succeeding Eleanor Barry, who had resigned to get married. Although she was privately familiar to a large and varied world of friends stretching all over the globe, she was known professionally to comparatively few – to the fashion trade by name, to her colleagues by sound and sight (the one described as 'a friendly roar', the other so unusual as to deserve a special description). To her fellow workers in the vineyard she was an object of admiration, affection and occasionally astonishment.

Two of these colleagues, oddly enough top members of the Opposition hierarchy, *Vogue* photographer and artist Sir Cecil Beaton and *Vogue* fashion editor Bettina Ballard, were the first to write about her. Each produced unforgettable vignettes: Sir Cecil in 1954 in *The Glass of Fashion* and Mrs Ballard in 1960 in her memoirs *In My Fashion*. To a larger audience Mrs Vreeland achieved instant, though anonymous, notoriety with her 'Why don't you ...?

features which became the most talked about and parodied pages of any fashion magazine. These offered such useful suggestions as 'Why don't you turn your old ermine coat into a bathrobe?', 'Why don't you rinse your blond child's hair in dead champagne?', 'Why don't you put all your dogs in yellow collars and leads?' (it's the 'all' that's so typical). There was even one – or was it a parody? – that asked, 'Why don't you wear a lighted Christmas tree in your hair?'

The features became God's gift to the New Yorker humourists, who made them so celebrated that they were being quoted a quarter of a century later and haunt her still. Mrs Vreeland dismisses them now as 'absurdities' (and indeed she may have had her pen near her cheek when she wrote some of them) but she justifies them as right in 1937, when a little fantasy and diversion did nobody any harm. When asked to revive them she refused. A spy in the office, Mrs Kaufman, collected such Vreelandisms as her now classic 'Pink is the navy blue of India', with which she regaled her husband, playwright George Kaufman, and his friend and sometime collaborator, Moss Hart. They gave Hart the idea of basing a play on the bizarre world of the *Bazaar*. *Lady in the Dark* played first on Broadway and then was made into a film in 1944. Mrs Vreeland, it has always been widely believed, was also the model for the part of the fashion editor in the film of *Funny Face* made in 1956.

Mrs Vreeland has continued to be written about increasingly since 1962 when she left the *Bazaar* to become editor-in-chief of *Vogue*. The rivalry between the two magazines had been so intense and well-known that this caused the same commotion as would the news that Tony Benn had joined the Tories or that Mr Carter had decided to run on a Republican ticket. The writing accelerated when ten years later she moved to the Metropolitan Museum of Art. Each reporter has tried to catch her specific quality, and all end in agreeing that she is *sui generis* – unique, a one-off shot. It is not only her personality that baffles definition; her looks are equally hard to describe. To Sir Cecil she resembled 'an authoritative crane'.

A British journalist likened her to a cassowary which sent readers running for their dictionaries where they found that a cassowary is a 'large running bird related to the ostrich'. More recently Truman Capote saw her as 'some extraordinary parrot'. Alongside such ornithological comparisons, she seems to inspire vegetable and zoological ones as well. Sir Cecil was reminded of 'cooked asparagus' by her suppleness in adapting to whatever piece of furniture on which she sat. Mrs Ballard wrote of 'her loping camel's gait with her long neck thrust forward like an inquisitive tortoise's.' Animal, vegetable, reptile or bird, these similes prove how difficult it is to put Mrs Vreeland's appearance into words. She is in fact a mass of highly imaginative mannerisms, behind which lurks for those whom she respects, admires or loves, a warm heart.

Having decided when she was young that she could not be pretty in the conventional sense, she set about inventing a way of looking. She made a virtue of her strong face with its commanding nose, broadening from a narrow bridge, her shining black eyes whose down-turned corners, unlike Walter Pater's Mona Lisa's, are less a little weary, more a little wary. On *Harper's Bazaar* she skinned back her longish hair (rinsed a dark blue) into a crocheted chenille snood topped by a crisp bow. She put her small feet in low-heeled, T- or ankle-strapped shoes. With her inevitable cigarette-holder, which she wields in her slim, long-fingered hand like a baton as if she were conducting her own performance, these added up to an instant identikit.

On *Vogue* she cut her hair, changed the colour to an unconvincing jet-black, but remained faithful to the shoes and cigarette-holder. There, as editor-in-chief, she religiously covered the Paris collections, setting a new level of courtesy by writing appreciative notes to the designers. And she also cossetted Seventh Avenue. At both, she was the arbiter whose approval was nervously sought. The *New Yorker* published a drawing of two journalists at a collection, the caption: 'Mrs Vreeland is frowning.'

She carries her personal ambience into her various offices and flats as a snail carries its house. Red is always a dominant colour – in cushions, curtains, walls, carpets – a colour she says she can't live without. Scent, whether from Floris vaporizer rings or Rigaud scented candles, is inevitable. So is a bulletin-board – at home thumbtacked with postcards and photographs of friends, at the office with clippings of pictures cut from newspapers or magazines which have caught her eye, or a quotation she wants to remember. In her *Vogue* office, the bulletin-board carried a quotation: 'Elegance is important, Courage and Dignity essential.'

Phyllis Lee Levin recalls at Mrs Vreeland's home, 'bowls of shells tossed with coral', and tables 'littered with silver fish'. Mrs Ballard remembered 'collections of Scotch snuff-boxes in horn or silver'. (Mrs Vreeland must have been the originator of the carefully composed 'careless clutter' which decorators were later to make a cliché of 'gracious living'.) All of this – along with bookshelves crammed with books and small objects, sofas massed with cushions, walls covered with pictures and sketches of herself by Augustus John, Bérand and Beaton – gave Sir Cecil himself the impression of 'a full room, almost a Victorianly stuffed room, but it does not seem so, for every last shell is polished and there is not a speck of dust . . .' To Mrs Ballard, Mrs Vreeland's surroundings suggested 'an overcrowded Turkish seraglio on a rather elegant boat'. Phyllis Lee Levin found the effect like 'a Matisse landscape, a Persian market and a gypsy camp by Bemelmans'. The result seems to have been somewhat overwhelming, but it is clear that Mrs Vreeland dominated her background.

As she re-creates her background with fidelity, she is equally constant to certain clothes which she repeats. In 1954 Sir Cecil sketched her wearing a tunic and slim black trousers; twenty-four years later at a party given for her in London she wore slim black trousers and a tunic, and looked just as slender and just as chic.

Like Barbara Cartland, she is a health fiend: massage (without which she said to Bettina Ballard 'I would walk on all fours'), vitamin injections, osteopathy – the lot. For both Mrs Cartland and Mrs Vreeland this regimen seems to have worked, for work hard and successfully they do. But Mrs Vreeland's stamina and energy may also have come from her parents. Her mother was American and her father, Scottish. His family name was Dalziel (pronounced DL, which may have given Diana the idea of pronouncing her name Deanne – that, or her childhood in Paris). In the seventeenth century Lord Carnwath (Carnwath was the Dalziel title, now, alas, extinct) had a daughter, thought to have been illegitimate, who served throughout the English Civil War as a Captain of Horse without, apparently, anybody's discovering her sex. Tam Dalziel – the family motto is 'I Dare' – became a mercenary in the Russian Army. He returned to Scotland at the time of the Restoration to serve under Charles II against the Covenanters. He was called 'Bloody Tam' because he is supposed to have introduced the thumbscrew. This extraordinary ancestry I have from a mutual Scottish friend, Christian, Lady Hesketh. She also added that the Dalziel coat of arms was a naked man on the gallows. 'It's not very usual,' she commented, 'to have a naked figure on a coat of arms.'

So far, neither the gallows nor the thumbscrews has surfaced in Mrs Vreeland. Anyway, the young Dalziels followed the fashionable route – London, Paris (where Diana was born), Cannes, Deauville, Biarritz. This peripatetic life made schooling necessarily erratic. The girls were put into school whenever and wherever their parents paused long enough, and removed when they were ready to move on. But a formal education was not needed. There was always Paris, where there exists a close and enriching relationship between the arts and society. Through her parents, Diana inhaled this heady atmosphere. To their house came Chaliapin, Nijinski, Diaghilev and especially the Castles. Europe was dance-mad and mad about the Castles. Diana remembers everybody dancing, the carpets rolled up and the victrola always going. But the rumblings of the approaching war could be heard above the gaiety, and the music had to stop.

The family came back to America in 1913. This meant New York and a series of proper girls' schools in which Diana must have seemed like a parakeet in a flutter of sparrows. 'They didn't know what to do with me,' she recalls – not really surprising as she spoke mostly French and knew very little English. So she ended up at the Folkine ballet school. America also meant Southampton and Wyoming, where the Dalziels took their children to escape the infantile paralysis epidemic, and where as a bonus they met Buffalo Bill. It was an action-packed life. Caught by the war the Dalziels stayed on. Diana made her debut in 1922 and in 1924, when she was eighteen, married tall, handsome, patrician T. Reed Vreeland. The ceremony took place, naturally, at society's pet church, St Thomas's on Fifth Avenue.

The young Vreelands' first five years were spent in Albany, New York – a strangely provincial town for an exotic – where their first son was born. (Their second son was born in America, too.) Reed Vreeland, having finished his apprenticeship at banking, was offered a place with the Guaranty Trust in London, and the family moved. London, however, was only a base for travels (although while there Mrs Vreeland apparently really did train with the Tiller Girls, a fact which was previously thought legendary). There was Paris, where Mrs Vreeland made friends with Chanel and later Christian Béraud, and satisfied her passion for clothes. The Vreelands skied in Austria, visited museums in Italy, listened to concerts in Salzburg. It was a period when those with a taste for luxury could satisfy it. It was not only the fabulous Mrs Lydig who could afford bench-made shoes. They and the finest silk hand-tucked monogrammed underwear and blouses as well as couture clothes were within the reach of the then almighty dollar.

The ever-darkening shadows of the Second World War brought the Vreelands, then in Switzerland, bag, baggage and offspring back to New York. It was at this point that Mrs Snow reached out for her. When, more than thirty years later, Mrs Vreeland was asked by Philippa Toomey of *The Times* why she accepted, she smiled her characteristically generous smile and answered, 'Money. Why, does anyone work for anything else?' As it turned out, she adored it. She loved being on *Vogue*, too and those who worked with her loved her. 'Her effect on the staff was electric,' said Grace Mirabella, then her assistant, now editor. 'Everything has an extra spark, an extra magic. She feels what's about to be going on and has the ability to project it.' Project it she did and in the Sixties not only transformed *Vogue* into an exciting magazine but, as Lally Weymouth wrote in *Rolling Stone* in 1977, into 'a chronicle of that extraordinary decade'. It was a startling and in many ways a sad and sick decade. And perhaps Mrs Vreeland's courageous reporting of it frightened the publishers. Or in a country where everything is aimed at an expensively-researched market, they felt that Mrs Vreeland's idiosyncratic method of editing ('I think', she said in an interview with the London *Sunday Times*, 'that what interests me will interest other women, what amuses me will amuse them') was not sufficiently representative. Whatever the reason, in 1971 Mrs Vreeland left, and magic left with her.

Being fired must have been a bitter blow, but she had already suffered a greater one. In 1967 her husband had died. She had loved him deeply and had made him the lodestar of her life. To work and work hard must have been a distraction from her grief, and suddenly she was deprived of that, too. But Mrs Vreeland was not a Dalziel for nothing. As she has often said, she hates the past, thinks only of the future. She set about picking up the pieces. At first she went out a lot, a flame for what *W* calls the 'Social Moths'. One of them explained, 'You see, she knows it is important to be seen.' Then she went abroad, following, perhaps unconsciously, a maxim attributed to Somerset Maugham that nothing so helps heal a broken heart as three thousand miles of water. On her return she found the Metropolitan Museum waiting on her doorstep. The rest is fashion history.

Needless to say, her office there is as usual painted red, but she is rarely in it, travelling both for herself and for her exhibitions. So far she has produced for the Costume Institute eight major exhibitions: 'The World of Balenciaga', 1972; 'The 10s, The 20s, The 30s: Inventive Clothes 1909–1939' (a selection of clothes from designers who in Mrs Vreeland's opinion were the most important influences of each decade), 1973; 'Romantic and Glamorous Hollywood Design', 1974: 'American Women of Style' (a galaxy of taste and wealth from Lady Mendl to Josephine Baker, planned to coincide with America's Bicentennial), 1975–6; 'The Glory of Russian Costume,' 1976; 'Vanity Fair' (a personal selection of items from the magnificent collection of the Metropolitan's Costume Institute), 1977; 'Diaghilev and the Ballets Russes', 1978; and the most recent and most regal, 'Fashions of the Hapsburg Era', opened 1979. Each exhibition has the strong flavour of her personal taste and convictions. What the Costume Institute calls her 'fabled flair' has made the opening nights of these exhibitions gala occasions, providing society columnists and fashion writers with delirious copy. They have attracted record attendances – 400,000 saw her second exhibition, and 'The Glory of Russian Costumes' nearly tripled that figure. New York newspapers burbled with superlatives. *The Times* even sent over from London their chief film critic, David Robinson, to New York for the Hollywood show, which he reported with knowledgeable enthusiasm. The 10s, the 20s and the 30s have been given a permanent life under the sub-title, *Inventive Clothes, 1909–1939*, in a book of spectacular photographs by Irving Penn with text by Mrs Vreeland, published both in New York and London (1977), as was 'The Glory of Russian Costume' under the title, *In the Russian Style* (1976).

In 1976, after the first Russian Exhibition, George Trow in the *New Yorker* magazine, discussing the public's reaction to the Vreeland exhibitions, wrote that they 'have had more influence on the attitude of New Yorkers to fashion than the last thirty-six issues of any fashion magazine'. It can be no coincidence that in July/August 1979 Yves Saint Laurent based his collection on the Ballets Russes, while Jules François Crahay for Lanvin called his *'Homage à Diaghilev'*. Truman Capote is quoted as saying that Mrs Vreeland 'has contributed more than anyone I can think of to the level of taste of American women.' With his usual humility he adds, '... She's a genius, but she's the kind of genius that very few people will ever recognize because you have to have genius yourself to recognize it.' Lady Hesketh says. 'I know that I shall have a morning of rejoicing when I am to see her.' Personally and professionally Mrs Vreeland adds pzazz to life.

Vreelandisms

About an American designer – 'My dear, no one but no one can touch his American look. .. Clothes with breezes running through their seams.'

From *In My Fashion* by Bettina Ballard

Instructing a hairdresser how she wanted a model about to be photographed to look – 'Twist the hair up, twist it out . . . way, way out, all the way to Outer Mongolia.'

From *In My Fashion* by Bettina Ballard

At the end of a rather dull collection by a great designer – 'My dear, these are clothes for a woman who goes nowhere and sees nobody.'

From *Tongue in Chic* by Ernestine Carter

Under the kleig lights at another collection on an August day, where the models danced and jigged until sweat ran down their unmade-up faces, Diana exclaimed – 'Lovely, like walking through a field with a fresh wind blowing on your face.'

From *Tongue in Chic* by Ernestine Carter

Heard at an Embassy party in London, where Mrs Vreeland was introduced to Jonathan Miller of 'Beyond the Fringe' fame, subsequently a doctor as well as a director and producer – 'Tell me, Dr Miller, what is *your* Holy Grail?'

Repeated to Lady Hesketh by a Social Moth who, picking Mrs Vreeland up at the Connaught Hotel in London, suggested walking the short distance to lunch at the Ritz overlooking Green Park – On arrival, she exclaimed 'My dear, how clever of you to find a hotel in the suburbs.'

aura
shley

LAURA ASHLEY

1926–

The Magic of Simplicity

One of the most unlikely figures to become a magic name is Laura Ashley. To begin with, she is the first to admit that what she produces is not fashion. Indeed, she insists upon it. In the second place, she is totally unlike any of the dazzling dragonflies that have paused for a minute on these pages. Although many of them originally came from small towns or villages, they soon acquired the sophisticated gloss of the capitals in which they found their fame. Mrs Ashley, despite her amazing success, retains the simplicity of her native Wales.

She was born in the mining-town of Merthyr Tydfil, incidentally also the birthplace of Mary Quant's father. The fresh country air she exudes is, however, less that of her coal-dusted birthplace than the peace of the small village of Machynlleth (where the Ashleys moved in 1961) and the beauty of the neighbouring town of Carno, both in Montgomeryshire. At the age of fifty-four Laura Ashley has the soft complexion, innocent of make-up, of a country woman and the friendly informality of a country neighbour. She is completely unself-conscious. Straight from her plane, *en route* from Vienna where the Ashleys had just opened a shop to the parent plant in Wales, she was unaware – and probably wouldn't have cared, anyway – that a strand of her reddish-brown hair had blown loose. She settles down to a mug of instant coffee, which she drinks with relish, and chats. She speaks of the perquisites of success (a success due, she emphasizes, in great part to her husband, Bernard, who is in her words, 'the driving force') with the guileless pleasure of a delighted child describing her newest toys.

These toys include an ocean-going yacht, an executive jet, an apartment in Brussels and a château in France. Perhaps this is because these signs of prosperity were not acquired as status symbols but each for a definite purpose. The yacht and the jet are for keeping in touch with their 70 shops in 12 countries and 10 factories in the UK, Holland, Eire, France and Holland, which they try to visit at least once a week. The apartment in Brussels is within easy reach of their European plants. The château in France – entirely furnished in Laura Ashley fabrics – provides a tax haven which their increasing affluence has made desirable.

All the other personalities in this book have begun their careers in some aspect of fashion. Mrs Ashley's early essays in design were a by-product of her husband's interest in silk-screen printing his own fabrics. They were married in 1950, and she had continued to work with the National Federation of Women's Institutes until the birth of her first child. (They now have four.) Perhaps it was the WI influence that led her first to small household objects: cotton table-mats, napkins, tea towels. The Ashleys printed these in their kitchen in Pimlico, where, in 1954, they founded their company. Laura sold them to handicraft shops and stores like Harrods and Heal's which had departments available for the sale of such items.

They had been baking the dyes in their oven, and pretty soon the oven was used more for hardening dyes than for cooking. The neighbours began to complain of the smell. In 1956 the Ashleys moved to Kent, converting into a factory an old coach-house in a romantic setting by the River Darent. However, disaster lurked behind the beauty; the river burst its banks and flooded the factory, submerging its contents. The Ashleys somehow struggled through, only to find themselves submerged once more in a rising tide of orders for their tea towels. It was but a step to add matching aprons and oven-gloves. The Ashley handwriting was beginning to emerge: prints with a rural flavour, natural and unaffected, in the colours of early spring leaves and flowers.

Success was on the horizon, but it did not come within reach until 1961, when they decided to move again, this time, at Mrs Ashley's instigation, to her native Wales. The search for suitable premises at a price they could afford took six weeks, during which Mrs Ashley and her children (by that time there were three) camped out. Then she found in the (for the non-Welsh) unpronouncable village of Machynlleth, three small cottages which could be made into one. The three cost £1,500, just about what the Ashleys could manage. (The cottages have since been replaced by a 500-acre farm with the equally unpronounceable name of 'Rhydoldog'.) In addition, one of the cottages already had a shop-front. This meant that they could sell directly as well as through stores.

Nearby, in a village called Carno, they found an abandoned dance-hall, which was quickly transformed into a factory. Here the Ashleys first dipped into clothing with a striped gardening-smock. Once launched, this took off like a rocket. As with many villages in Wales, Carno's small population was mostly out of work, except for occasional seasonal jobs of haymaking and sheep-shearing. They longed for security, and the Ashleys and their gardening smock gave it to them. Carno began to enjoy the fruits of full employment. Soon more room was needed, and the Ashleys found another disused building – this time a railway station with a large shunting shed faced in local granite. There they employed in 1977 400 people. In 1979 their employees in Wales totalled over 1,000.

The Ashleys were on their way. In 1979 their exports came to £4,500,000. (In 1977 they had won the Queen's Award for Export Achievement, and the Ashleys were received by Her Majesty on the royal yacht *Brittania.*) In 1979 their world-wide turnover was £25,000,000. It is only fair to say that the number of shops and factories given varies from day to day; even as this is being written a new shop has been opened – their first Children's Shop. For these they prefer what Mrs Ashley calls 'the beautiful cities', and their sites read like a grand tour: London, Edinburgh, Bath, Cheltenham, Cambridge, Norwich, Oxford, Paris, Aix en Provence, The Hague, Munich and so on. They choose the right areas – never the obvious shopping ones – in Washington it's Georgetown, in Boston it's Back Bay, in Edinburgh it's George Street. Typical of their enlightened self-interest is their selection for their shops of old buildings in need of restoration. For example, in Guildford they chose the seventeenth-century Old Cloth Hall; in Shrewsbury, Wyle cop, a street of medieval houses; and in Vienna a thirteenth-century building, rebuilt 300 years ago after a fire. They use local architects, but Mr Ashley designs the interiors in keeping with the simple farmhouse mood – lots of polished oak, often from their farm, no frills – which the Ashleys have made their own. The shops which combine home furnishings (these account for more than half their sales) and clothes, have a homey atmosphere. 'People want to be comforted,' Mrs Ashley thinks, and she was amused when a New York journalist said, after visiting the Madison Avenue shop, that she would have liked to be asked to stay for tea.

Despite their constant expansion, the Ashleys keep in touch with Carno, visiting the plant at least once a week. An eight-page newsletter keeps them in touch with all their employees and also keeps the staff up to date with future Ashley plans. One celebrating their Silver Jubilee, beside the usual house-organ news items, notes the expansion of ranges in clothing, wallpapers and fabrics, new projects – collapsible lampshades, floor and wall tiles, a fragrance developed by Mr Ashley, plans and places for new shops and, unexpectedly, the sale of small scraps from the cutting tables in one-kilo bags for patchwork. 'I adore patchwork,' says Mrs Ashley, 'and we want to do something for our customers.' The Ashleys also like to do something for the communities where their shops are situated. For the Bath Festival of 1978/9, they sponsored the Vivaldi Tercentenary celebrations.

Although Mrs Ashley thinks they are very enclosed – they have their own factories, their own print works, their own shops – this monolithic structure enables them to keep prices down; but a disadvantage to her is that they get no criticism except from the customers themselves. 'What doesn't sell is ruthlessly pruned out,' she says. 'The customers show what they don't like by what they don't buy. In that way they tell me what they want.' This is why Mrs Ashley studies the sales analyses, happily she adores figures.

The Ashleys are also a very close family operation. Three of the children are in the company: Jane, 26, who went to the Chelsea College of Art, takes the publicity photographs ('She catches the mood of my thinking,' says her mother); David, 25, trained as an engineer, runs the marketing operation; Nick, 23, photographs the house furnishings. The youngest, Emma, 14, was allowed to design the brightly-coloured (a departure for the Ashleys) dungarees that, as Bernadine Morris wrote in the *New York Times*, were the 'eye-popping finale' to the Ashleys' New York show.

Mrs Ashley finds it interesting that two such sophisticated centres as New York and Vienna are the most conservative. 'They want our turn-of-the-century things – the pinafores, the long dresses, the frilly blouses and nightdresses.' Of course, clothes such as these were the basis of her original success and show off to the best advantage the unaffected charm of her sprigged milkmaid prints. Their freshness is a conscious reaction against the noise, brutality and impersonality of big cities – the hoodlums and drug addicts, the general aggro. 'I have a strong streak of Puritanism,' Mrs Ashley confesses. 'I was pushed into designing, but through designing I express my feelings.'

These feelings happened to coincide with a change of mood in fashion. Women were beginning to be sick of the decadent pastiches of the Thirties, the Art Deco tat, the second-hand clothes lark. They were ready for the clean country look of a more innocent past. Laura Ashley was the answer.

As for fashion, she says with no false humility, 'We just produced something as an alternative to jeans. What we make is not fashion.' When the Ashleys were in America on a surveying trip, they stayed at the British Embassy in Washington where, as it happens, the State bedroom has been re-decorated in Laura Ashley fabrics. Lady Henderson, the British Ambassadress, accompanied the Ashleys to New York where she opened their Madison Avenue shop. Afterwards Lady Henderson took Mrs Ashley on to the Zandra

Rhodes showing. Mrs Ashley was breathless: 'So beautiful,' she sighed. 'That was fashion.'

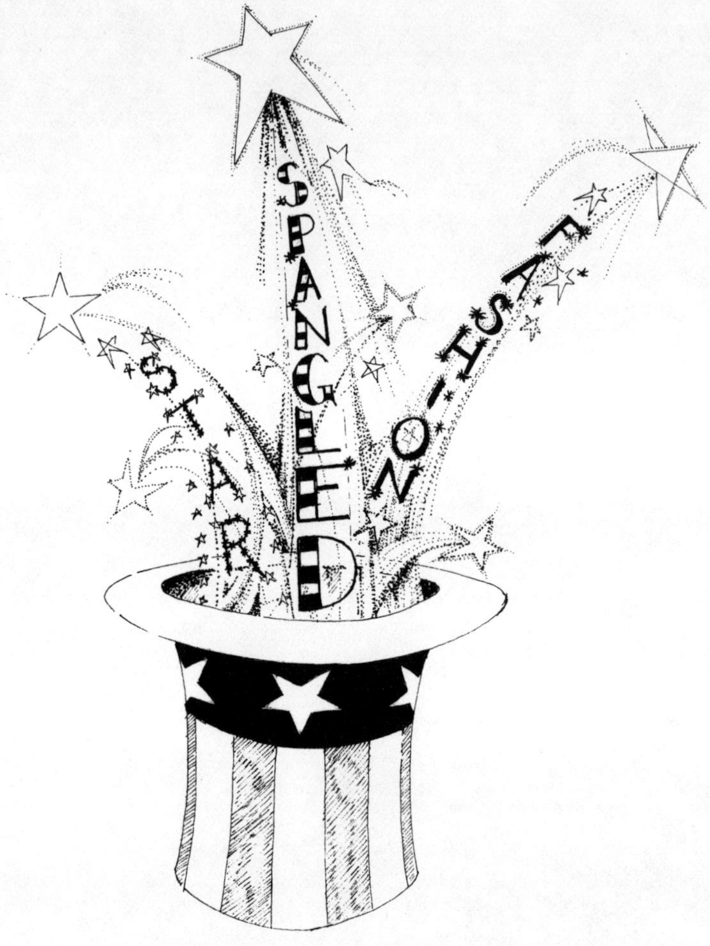
STAR
SPANGLED
FASHION

CLAIRE McCARDELL

1905–1958

BONNIE CASHIN

190 ?–

CALVIN KLEIN

1942–

Star Spangled Magic

There is a special magic about American fashion. It has as many facets as there are stars and stripes. There are the giants of the trade: Norman Norell, James Galanos, Pauline Trigère, whose names are too established to need further commendation. There are the designers who produce suavely packaged interpretations of European inspiration, cleverly adapted to the American taste. There are the designers who have evolved a peculiarly American blend of well-made, glamorous and becoming clothes. And there are the designers who have either created or caught a distinctive American look which could be loosely described as easy: clothes imbued with a specific kind of contemporary informality. It is invidious to name only a few from the hotbed of talents which this vast country nourishes, and even more invidious to select from those in the second category. In the third there are the reliable and enduring Bill Blass from Indiana, Dominican-born Oscar de la Renta and the comparative late-comer, Halston from Iowa.

Each of these three possesses high talents and has achieved success as well as kudos. Each has mastered a high standard of ready-to-wear production. All appeal to the upper income group, the Beautiful People: Blass with a sure sense of refinement, de la Renta with a dramatic impact, Halston with a style of apparent simplicity – the kind that, costing a packet, becomes a status symbol. His clothes are not always easy to wear, demanding as they do perfect shapes to wear them properly. As one disgruntled manufacturer put it, 'Halston dresses bodies, not women.' All three are good-looking, all are society pets, mingling with, and entertaining, the people they dress – and Halston is the biggest party-giver of them all. Each of these names has its magic, but there are three in the last category, two women and a man, who seem to express most potently a purely American idiom. They are the late Claire McCardell, Bonnie Cashin and the youngest and most recent, Calvin Klein.

Claire McCardell, in her short life (she died at the tragically early age of fifty-three), made an indelible mark. Tall, slim, blonde, with a generous smile that extended to her eyes, she was born in Maryland in 1905, came to New York to study at what was later to be called the Parson's School of Design and stayed on to become one of America's most loved and distinguished designers. Her individual talent flowered during the last war, which isolated American fashion from Paris, up until then its major source of inspiration. America, like England, was frozen in the pre-war Schiaparelli silhouette – nipped-in waists, narrow skirts, wide padded shoulders. Because of a national tendency toward exaggeration – and also a natural wish to provide novelty – designers first stretched the shoulders even farther out and then padded them up to ear height, producing what looked like some sort of grotesque deformity. Carmel Snow recalled the remark made by the American humourist Frank Sullivan when he had his first glimpse of this pugnacious silhouette: 'You slap your uncle on the shoulder and find it's your aunt.' Miss McCardell was the first designer to discard the pads. Her softly curved or dropped shoulders, with sleeves cut in one with the bodice or deep arm-holed, pre-dated Christian Dior's. She was to pre-date him again when, just after the war in 1946, she made dresses with full circular skirts dropping below calf-length a year before the debut of the New Look.

Wartime restrictions were no hardship for Miss McCardell. She had a natural affinity for what were considered 'poor' fabrics: cotton, seersucker, voile, dotted Swiss calico, mattress ticking, wool jersey. In *The Wheels of Fashion* Phyllis Lee Levin describes the dismay of one of the *Harper's Bazaar* copy-writers, Alice Morris, at having to write a caption for a photograph of one of Claire McCardell's just-after-the-war dresses. It was not only padless; it had a narrow-shouldered, high-waisted, fitted bodice, full skirt, three-quarter sleeves, and it was made of cotton. Miss Morris, as was usual at *Harper's Bazaar*, fled to fashion editor Diana Vreeland for help. 'Tell me,' she asked, 'what's so great about this dress?' Mrs Vreeland gave one of her penetrating, if mysterious, replies. 'But, Alice, it's wonderful. It's so pathetic.' Miss Morris, tactfully translating 'pathetic' into 'frugal', realized that Mrs Vreeland was right as usual. Miss McCardell had initiated a new and important direction for fashion.

One of Miss McCardell's most far-reaching successes with unpretentious materials was with denim. She first used it in 1943 for a capacious wrap-around coverall which Lord and Taylor christened the Popover – a play of words on an American muffin, hollow within, which, when risen, pops over the baking tin. According to Sally Kirkland, Miss McCardell's most perceptive biographer, 75,000 Popovers were sold and with them a quarter of a million yards of denim. As for denim, it is with us still in the omnipresent jeans. The ballet proved an unexpected source of inspiration for Miss McCardell. Just as she hated padded shoulders and padded bras, she liked flat-heeled shoes, partly because they suited her free and easy clothes and partly because during the war real shoes were rationed. In 1944 she found the answer in ballet slippers with the result that the firm of Capezio, makers of ballet shoes, found itself in the real shoe business as well. In 1943 Miss McCardell had introduced leotards. For several reasons they were not successful at the time (*Life* called them 'funny tights'), but they were the direct ancestors of the Birthday Suit (1962), the Body-Stocking (1965), the knitted cat-suit (1968) and even perhaps of tights (1958). In 1978 they came back as leotards.

'Timeless' has become a cliché, but that Miss McCardell's clothes are timeless was proven when in 1972 a retrospective showing of her clothes, both at the Fashion Institute of Technology in New York and the Los Angeles County Museum, got rave reviews from *Newsweek* and the *New York Times*. *Newsweek* wrote, 'By any yardstick it was the smash fashion collection of the season.' The *Times* wrote, 'These are styles that can be worn today.' If that was true of 1972, it is equally true of 1979.

Miss McCardell was an Easterner. Another completely indigenous designer sprang from the West Coast, Californian Bonnie Cashin. As small as Miss McCardell was tall, Miss Cashin has eyes the deep blue of the Pacific Ocean, while Miss McCardell's were the green-blue of the Atlantic near which she grew up. Dress design came naturally to Miss Cashin, for her mother had made custom-built clothes. But Miss Cashin's horizons stretched far beyond the usual boundaries of fashion, surrounded as she was by a father who was an artist and inventor, an uncle who was a geophysicist, and a mathematician brother. Her own interest in the arts (she studied painting at the Art Students' League in New York) has made her more at home in the company of artists, museum directors and writers than in the society-cum-fashion world. After a stint in a New York wholesale house, she returned to California in 1943, to Hollywood, where she designed the clothes for her first film, *Claudia*, made that year. This was followed by *Laura* and *A Tree Grows in Brooklyn*, both made in 1944. In all, she designed clothes for thirty-three films in six years, ranging from modern dress as for *Laura*, razzle-dazzle for *Billy Rose's Diamond Horseshoe*, 1945, to period costume for *Anna and the King of Siam*, 1946. Her last film was *Give My Regards to Broadway* in 1948, and the next year she was on her way, if not to Broadway, to New York.

There in 1949 she started designing clothes and almost at once won a Coty Award and a Neiman-Marcus Award, both in 1950. Encouraged – and who wouldn't be? – she opened her own design studio in 1953. Miss Cashin was one of the first to foresee the effects of the great hegira of the young marrieds from a city which had become too dangerous and difficult in which to bring up children. She perceived that this exurbanite living would require special fashions – clothes that would suit the country but also be at home in the city. Where other designers design, as they say, 'for a purpose' (a wedding dress, a sports dress or a grand occasion dress), Bonnie Cashin designs for a way of life. 'You have to fit into your environment,' she says. That includes an understanding of the influence of architecture, as it creates rooms with low ceilings and minimal cupboard space; of air travel, where a few hours' flight can mean a dramatic difference in temperature; the frenetic pace of contemporary life. 'Some people,' she said in 1966 with sincere concern, 'don't look like the twentieth century.'

Although her clothes have changed subtly over the years, the principle behind her designs has remained the same. Their appearance is an amalgam of where she has lived, where she has worked, where she has travelled and what she has seen. From Western ranch life came her ponchos (long before they were part of Hippy gear), boots (as early as 1944), fringed suedes (long before the Red Indian fringes became a symbol of social protest in the late Sixties). From the Chinese influence prevalent on that coast came the genesis of the layered look: beginning with a 'fat man's vest', a loose sleeveless jacket, and the Chinese 'No' coat 'cut to hang naturally'. These had developed by 1960 into a complete system of 'layers', a good decade-and-a-half before this look hit Europe. Miss Cashin has continued with this theory of dressing which in her hands is like a striptease in reverse. A typical layered outfit of 1966 starts with a cashmere shift, its funnel neck stretching into a hood at will, over which could be added a full skirt of thick wool, and over these an unlined wool three-quarter-length tunic-jacket split at the sides, and over all a blanket poncho.

Characteristic McCardell signatures were a Phelps leather belt and a swinging shoulder-bag; typical Cashin ones are a generous 'Cashin Carry' leather tote bag, leather bindings and 'hardware' fastenings. Long before 'ecology' and 'organic' became part of the vocabulary, Miss Cashin preferred 'natural' rather than synthetic fibres: cashmere, tweed, wool, wool jersey, leather, suede, mohair (which she was the first to use as a dress fabric) and even candlewick. These may sound sober but in Miss Cashin's hands they sing with colour: geranium red, violet, curry, green tea. She has designed almost everything that can be made of leather except shoes. In 1964 she tried her hand at sweaters for the famous Scottish firm of Ballantyne; in 1972 she set up her own 'Knittery'. Being a professional, she always starts from scratch, studying the machines in order to know – often far better than the tradition-bound operators – what they can do and then does it.

All the designers mentioned in this chapter have reached the height of Coty Awards' Hall of Fame, but Bonnie Cashin also has other distinctions. She has been given two retrospective shows (Miss McCardell had one, too, but it was, alas, posthumous). The first Cashin retrospective was in 1962 at the Brooklyn Museum, which had been collecting her clothes since 1950; the second was in 1966 in London, put on by *Time/Life*. In 1960 Miss Cashin had been the first American designer to be given her own corner in a London store, Liberty's, where her clothes can still be found.

All of Miss Cashin's few inches quiver like a humming-bird with enthusiasm, with the excitement of new projects. A pet phrase is 'I'm on a new plateau', which means she is about to embark on another challenging venture. But in every aspect of fashion which she tackles, the handwriting emerges triumphantly as her own.

Miss McCardell's clothes have been called timeless – and rightly. So are Miss Cashin's. There are those in London who still wear her coats dating from 1960.

The United States of America with its varied climate, varied cultures, melting-pot population, is united in one thing – if not always in others. It is in love with the new. And the newest star in fashion is Calvin Klein – that rare thing, a New Yorker by birth. His leap to the top described in 1976 by Eleanor Lambert in *World of Fashion* as 'one of the most sensational successes in recent fashion history'. A graduate of the Fashion Institute of Technology, he left with his diploma in 1962. After five years free-lance designing for various manufacturers, he set up in 1967 under his own name. Recognition came swiftly, if not with quite the speed of Miss Cashin's. In 1973 he received his first Coty Award, in 1974 a Coty Return Award, and by 1975 he was, at thirty-three, in the Hall of Fame. He soon began to hold an almost equally coveted position in full colour on the front cover of *W*. An issue of that paper in 1979 devoted to 'Temptations' includes a full-page photograph of Mr Klein. Although it bears no identification other than his name and that of the photographer, Arthur Elgort, it is presumably an advertisement, for this technique of promotion is often to be found on *W*'s pages – cost $4,910 (in colour it would be $6,910). Mr Klein is wearing a simple open-necked shirt which sets off his interesting pallor as his softly-fluffed hair (perhaps due to a deft blow-dry, who knows?) sets off his direct gaze and sensitive mouth. It is a romantic photograph showing Mr Klein as suitably ensconsed among the 'Temptations'. That photograph appeared in June, and in black and white. Two months later (and $2,000 more) Mr Klein was in colour, a sun-tanned young man, all rugged informality.

First known for this sportswear, he is now equally known for what *W* call his 'sexy nightdresses'. *W*, not unknown for inuendo, may have meant to imply that these made their wearers look bedworthy, but in fact they are not bedwear but what used to be called, pre-*W*, 'evening dresses'. Still there is no doubt that they are sexy.

Different in every other way from Claire McCardell, Mr Klein, in his easy clothes, shows himself as her lineal descendant. Even the rolled-up sleeves of his informal cotton-knit tunic-shirts of 1976 echo the turned-back sleeves of Miss McCardell's revolutionary 'Popover' of thirty-three years before. The broad Rothko-esque bands of contrasting colour at the hems of his 1979 sports skirts may be a distant echo of Yves Saint Laurent 1946 Moroccan; the interpretation is his own.

British *Vogue* in its retrospective (as opposed to 'retro', American for nostalgic fashion) summing-up of the Seventies calls Calvin Klein the 'King of Unclutter'. That only partly explains his very personal style, as does the over-used phrase 'pared down'. He himself told Ann Boyd of the *Observer* that he 'hated unnecessary trimmings'. What results is a paradox, a sophisticated negligence which carries even into his essay in gold lamé – a straight three-quarter-length falling jacket over black pants. It carries through to the leathers and suedes he has designed for Gianni Versace – soft suede cardigans, hanging loose or kimono-sleeved and wrapped over, triple-belted in soft leather thongs, or equally soft chamois tops and trousers, the tops belted in leather. These swathed thong belts, wrapped or twisted, have become a Klein signature – whether in leather or in plaited twine. In fabric, he combines prints and stripes with easy virtuosity, handles *crêpe de Chine*, that most difficult of fabrics, printed or double-faced in contrasting colour, with authority.

The Klein nonchalance and casualness is somewhat deceptive. Like Halston's clothes, which seem as smoothly-flowing as a ballerina's gesture, they are not as easy to wear as they look, although Klein has taken a tip from Chanel and provides pockets, not only woman's best friends but an easy method of achieving the desired stance to show off the dress to its best advantage. Again like Halston his jewellery is especially designed for him. In 1972 Halston made Elsa Peretti's jewellery a compulsory fashion accessory; in 1979 Klein uses Bonwillum to bring back long strings of gilt beads and hoop ear-rings.

Calvin Klein, now thirty-eight, has raised the look of careless ease, which is America's unique contribution to fashion, to a new level. He has given the runabout a Rolls Royce finish.

YVES SAINT LAURENT

1936–

The Magic of Now

Yves Saint Laurent is one of the most difficult of designers to analyze or summarize. His career has been, until the mid-Seventies, a series of dazzling ups and downs, of inspirational back-ings and forth-ings. His talent is indubitable, his charm incontestable (his first friends, associates and supporters are still with him, loyal to a man or woman), the intensity of his dedication unquestioned – as Pierre Bergé has said on two occasions, 'Yves was born with a nervous breakdown.' What makes him so hard to sum up is a teasing question. Perhaps it is because at forty-four he is not, as someone said of Alfred de Musset, '... a young man with his future behind him' – it lies straight ahead; at least one hopes it is now straight. All that jumping about in time and place from idea to ideology is pretty confusing in retrospect.

As always the best place to start is at the beginning. Yves Saint (never St) Laurent was born in Oran, Algeria, of French parents. In 1954 he was taken on by the late Christian Dior when he was a shy, spectacled eighteen-year-old, a novice without any experience, armed only with a recommendation from Michel de Brunhoff, editor of French *Vogue* and inspired talent-spotter. That was a dramatic enough start for any first act, and Saint Laurent's career to date has been divided into three. Saint Laurent worked modestly behind the scenes in the atelier, known to the French journalists, who ferret out every secret corner of the great Couture Houses and nose out the skeletons behind every cupboard door, but largely unknown to the foreign press until Dior's death in 1957. Then, like the circus performer bursting through the paper ring, he appeared as Dior's successor. Here was a twenty-one year old inheriting, after only three years of working with the Master, the mantle of an acknowledged genius of fifty-one, who had made the name of the House of Dior world famous. The mantle was indeed a heavy one. Besides the terrifying challenge of succeeding success, there rested on Saint Laurent's slender shoulders the burden of a massive organization and an equally massive investment.

Paris held its breath and let it out with a great gust of relief when Saint Laurent's first collection in 1958 produced his immediately successful Trapeze line. (It was to become the classic maternity dress shape – and remain so for years.) It had been whispered that the young man might not be able to withstand 'Le Team' – the trio of formidable women, Mesdames Marguerite, Raymonde and Bricard, who had been the great man's right hands. In fact the ladies rallied and produced for their new star an impeccable production in the finest Dior tradition of exquisite finish and perfect marriage of accessories. (It was later to be seen that Saint Laurent needed no lessons in accessorizing.) Strong men and stronger women wept as they fought their way past photographers, waiters with trays of champagne perilously balanced and frenzied friends of the House, to embrace the new hero. Paris is so enamoured of fashion that a large crowd had gathered in the Avenue Montaigne, and to satisfy their acclaim, the reluctant and overwhelmed young man was propelled on to a balcony to wave, like British Royalty, to his admirers.

All seemed roses, but there were thorns. The administration had been used to Dior's masterly understanding of buyer mentality – always subtly revising some lines from the previous collection to reassure them, dropping in a foretaste of the line to come, thus gently preparing them, and prepared himself to withdraw or adapt according to market reaction. Thus they were uneasy when Saint Laurent proceeded to ring up the curtain on an entirely different scene each season. The Dior tradition also demanded an inordinate number of models (often nearly two hundred), too many for Saint Laurent's budding talent. (He was by 1976 to knock off three hundred.) Timing is the essence of leadership; it is more fatal to be too soon than too late – and Saint Laurent's timing was distinctly askew. In his second collection he dropped his skirts to calf-length and even lower for late day, about ten years too soon. The French press were outraged and turned against their hero with the same vehemence with which they had hailed him six months before. When the next year (1959) Saint Laurent hobbled his skirts above the knees, they were even more irate. 'Dresses which proclaim novelty at any price put up the audience's backs when they are first shown' was a maxim of Christian Dior which proved to be all too true by the outburst which greeted Saint Laurent's short skirts, too soon, alas, by five years. Unease gave way to nervousness. The House had too much at stake – its by-products were so multitudinous that American journalists were apt to refer to it as 'the General Store'.

The climax was reached in July 1960 when Saint Laurent showed his Beat Collection. This was not only at the wrong time but in the wrong place. He was in a way hoisted by his own inherited petard: the perfect execution, the flawless production, the ambience of scented luxury, which were all wrong for King's Road inspired clothes. So also were the lavish fabrics. A Rocker's leather jacket interpreted in crocodile, fox-edged, informal cardigans intricately knitted in ribbon and trimmed with fur seemed perverse. This was the end. Saint Laurent was released for military service. It did not need subsequent events to show how premature the panic was. Among the ideas which had shocked the establishment were some which were to last for years: the fur jacket with knitted sleeves and polo neck (the beginning of Saint Laurent's successful jumper look) among them. The curtain came down on Act I of the drama.

Act II began on a melancholy note. Delicate and highly-strung, Saint Laurent was patently unsuited to army life and was shortly invalided out. In the meantime, Paris was indulging in an orgy of sides-taking and speculation as Saint Laurent and the House of Dior sued and counter-sued. Soon it was rumoured that Saint Laurent was planning to open on his own. *Women's Wear Daily*, which had espoused his cause, began a massive build-up, but it was that incredible fixer, a female Rudolf Kommer, Marie-Louise Bousquet, who made it possible. She introduced Saint Laurent to Pierre Bergé. Pierre Bergé's reputation had been made an entrepreneur of the painter Bernard Buffet, whom he had steered to unforeseen heights of fame and fortune. It was Bergé who found the first financial backer for the new House – J. Mack Robinson, a financier from as far away as Atlanta, Georgia, USA. It was Bergé who has guided Saint Laurent through the years to his present pre-eminence where not only is his name magic but his initials as well. At the beginning some saw Bergé as a Svengali. If so, it is clear he is a benevolent one and, perhaps most important, one who knows how to handle this delicately-balanced talent.

Saint Laurent, diffident and unassuming, with the beautiful manners peculiar to well-brought-up young French boys, had made many friends at Dior. When the projected plan was on its way to becoming a reality, defectors wore a path from the Maison Dior to the pretty little house in Passy, a smart residential neighbourhood and as far as Saint Laurent could get from the Avenue Montaigne without actually leaving Paris. Victoire, Christian Dior's favourite model, led the way, followed by chief vendeuse Yvonne de Peyerimhoff, as fair as Victoire was dark, and husky-voiced Suzanne Luling from Dior's village of Granville, who had been his intimate associate from the start, with a finger in every pie.

One of the reasons for taking the little Passy villa must have been its miniature but graceful curving staircase. For reasons which escape journalists, Society and celebrities vie for invitations to the press showings of the couture, and ever since Chanel the staircase had been not only a vantage-point from which to see collections but a place of honour on which the Great are happy to be squeezed like sardines. For this opening Saint Laurent sensibly eschewed the gigantic flower arrangements customary in the high-ceilinged salons of Houses like Dior – impressive to the guests but often oppressive to the journalists who occasionally have to peer through branches and blooms like animals in a Rousseau jungle. Instead, he tastefully disposed around the two small rooms Madame Rubinstein (always first to patronize a new – and talked about –

talent), Zizi Jeanmaire, dancer and friend, along with some French titles and a Guinness or two. Eventually the staircase was to be crowded with notables, including Paloma Picasso, and, acting as his *mannequins de ville*, his friends, Marisa Berenson, granddaughter of Schiaparelli, who married American James Baldwin in 1976, and Lulu de la Falaise, daughter of Maxime, since 1977 married to Thadée Kossowski and very much part of the YSL scene, each wearing her Saint Laurent clothes from the current collection with infectious delight. Inventive and sometimes overpowering plant arrangements appeared. For the African Collection of 1967 a jungle was contrived of palms, orchids, bananas, paw paws, pineapples and exotic leaves. The next year for his protest collection flowers were replaced by a sculpture by Cézar.

At the first collection in 4 February 1962, the small salons were packed to the gills so tightly that journalists found themselves writing on their neighbours' notebooks. In the front row was the entire staff of *Women's Wear Daily*; in the back rows, it had to be assumed, were legless torsos. The build-up had been too great; the let-down was inevitable. Perhaps a reaction to his recent dramas, the collection surprised only by its sobriety, showing if any influence, that of Balenciaga. Still there was to be perceived – and applauded – what became typical of Saint Laurent: the fantastic accessorizing for which he has a special talent. And it was the first glimpse of his famous pea jacket, to which he remained faithful through many seasons. The success of the collection was assured, for it had been bought *en bloc* before its showing by Fortnum and Mason in London and several other stores overseas. Their buyers were still wreathed in smiles at his porters' smocks in his second collection, and were even happier at his third. Balenciaga had been replaced by a tribute to Saint Laurent's late patron, Dior – the lilies of the valley (Dior's lucky flower), the lingerie touches Dior loved for spring, the delicate femininity which was Dior's hallmark. The inspiration may have been Dior; its interpretation was pure Saint

Laurent, as were the pinafore dresses with contrasting sleeves, both for day and evening.

In Saint Laurent's collection of August 1963 he reverted to his basic Balenciaga suit shape but followed all Paris into boots and patterned stockings. He accoutred the suits with dramatic accessories: the highest boots in booted Paris, Robin Hood hats, Maid Marian medieval evening dresses. To the British this was Sherwood Forest, while the French were busy scribbling Louis Onze, François Villon, Joan of Arc. It was all great fun, except for the buyers whose view was one that they were to repeat in almost the same words in 1968: 'When you take off the garnish, what's left we bought before – and our customers won't want the garnish.' This gave a certain credence to a theory that Saint Laurent was at heart an inspired boutique designer who could transform a familiar shape by means of imaginative accessories. Indeed, years later in 1976, he said, 'Accessories are extremely important today. They have become almost more important than clothes.' Fortunately by then, buyers had become indoctrinated. The strong medieval flavour of the collection was the first sign of another Saint Laurent characteristic: the need for a theme from history, art, literature or current events.

True to form, in his next collection in 1964, Saint Laurent discarded his manly rustic swagger for what his hand-out described as a collection for 'the young, delicate, dainty fragile woman'. For this ideal, he created a deliciously feminine wardrobe, as beguiling as the Watteau or Fragonard shepherdesses who may have inspired him – and as delightfully artificial.

In August of that year, he did another *volte face*. At a moment when all couture was following Courrèges's lead of 1963 and contesting his title for the shortest skirts in Paris, Saint Laurent dropped his to mid-calf length, or lower for late day. This was his second attempt, and once more his timing was wrong. He showed the same week that Courrèges scored a triumph with skirts shorter than ever, the most subtly-tailored trouser-suits for day and the most daring for evening. Against the youthful vigour and gaiety of this collection, and with all the rest of the couture also on a youth kick, Saint Laurent's long skirts looked middle-aged and dowdy. The Press was not impressed.

Perhaps because of the poor reviews which tended to discourage buyers, Saint Laurent announced in 1965 that he would join Balenciaga and Givenchy, who for the same reasons had delayed showing to the press until the buyers had seen the collection and, it was hoped, bought. Unfortunately, his pique had provoked him into making some intemperate remarks which the French and American journalists took poorly. They showed their resentment by staying away from his collection in droves. This was not the object of the exercise nor can it have been very encouraging to Mr Richard Salomon, Chairman of Lanvin-Charles of the Ritz, who had that year bought out Mr Robinson for a reputed million dollars. 'Urbane' is the adjective generally applied to Mr Salomon, and he succeeded in persuading Saint Laurent to change his mind. He returned to the fold in 1966 but indicated his reluctance by not showing until five days later than his colleagues, thus keeping journalists tapping their feet impatiently. It was not until after Balenciaga's retirement in 1969 that Saint Laurent and Givenchy came into line.

Actually, those who stayed away had cut off their noses to spite their pages, for the Saint Laurent August collection turned out to include two headliners: the first was a group of fur coats, the fur used in horizontal bands alternating with strips of ciré or suede – a new and ingenious idea that was still being copied a decade later. Beneath these coats were the second – white jersey shifts which also made fashion history. Some had black bars and carefully-spaced squares of red and yellow. These were his Mondrian dresses. Others bore the jagged abstract shapes in red, purple and green typical of Poliakoff. The Mondrian dresses were the talk of Paris, but, alas, you can't win for winning. The buyers' verdict was, 'They're wonderful, but they'll be copied so fast it's no use buying them.' They were right. Still the publicity they reaped put Saint Laurent firmly in the public eye.

Six months later, in January 1966, he dropped art for anchors. As one onlooker remarked, 'Last year Saint Laurent's mother gave him a book on Mondrian; this year she must have given him a yacht.' Of the nautical outfits, the greatest success were the jaunty blazers, a theme he was to return to, and the pants, a theme he was to enlarge upon. The collection was memorable for the first appearance of joke brides, a form of drollery he was to continue into the next decade. The Bride, the traditional end of couture collections, usually embodies what the designer considered his most important theme. To laugh at a Bride was like laughing in church. Saint Laurent's Brides were frankly gimmicks. For this life on the bounding waves collection his Bride, instead of carrying her bouquet, was herself the bouquet, enveloped in a florist's cornucopia of white organdie filled with flowers, their stalks the model's own bare legs. She processed to bird song – twitterings, no gulls.

Back on land in his next collection of 1966, Saint Laurent had turned to Pop Art: a Lichtenstein-type nude silhouetted down one side of a black shift, puffed-out red lips across the bosom of another, and other surrealist trimmings reminiscent of Schiaparelli. This time his Bride was in keeping with the Pop Art mood with a bouquet which was part of her dress – an arum lily appliquéd on the front, its plastic bloom holding a lighted electric bulb just under her chin. The Pop Art overshadowed the two most important points of the collection. One was the first appearance of his 'smoking'; the other his bow to *Dr Zhivago*, which had put the whole couture on the steppes of Russia. He may not then have realized that, having caught the Russian bug, it would, like the malaria germ, stay always in his blood. Nor did he apparently anticipate the success of his 'smoking' transformed into 'city pants' the next year, for Saint Laurent continued to pursue his career as if it were a play with a series of independent scenes but from the enthusiasts always sure of a standing ovation.

He had his personal hang-ups, like his admiration for Chanel (which was returned), whose signatures – the shot cuffs, the pearls, the chains, the fake gardenias – turned up over and over again, dropped in, as it were, in 1964, 1967 and 1968; his curious partiality for Lord Fauntleroy suits, which appeared in 1965 and 1966. Pop Art, Mondrian and social awareness were also peculiar to him. On the other hand, he would sniff the same breeze as his fellows in couture, occasionally at the same time (as with boots and Dr Zhivago) often after, but with a dramatic projection which made his interpretations, even if late, outshine their predecessors. For example, his transparent dresses of 1966, beaded only at strategic points, were late-comers in the trend toward nudity which had begun in 1963 with plunging necklines and continued on to bare midriffs, cut-outs (at Cardin as numerous as the holes in a Gruyère cheese), thigh-high slit skirts and see-through dresses. The surprise of Saint Laurent's, was due in part to the fact that they were done by this notoriously shy young man. When in 1968 he went even farther and showed a transparent black chiffon tent, ostrich-girdled at the necessary point, followed by a completely transparent shirt above strictly tailored shorts, he was pipped at the post as far as sensation went by Courrèges, who topped his daisy-appliquéd hipster shorts with two of the daisies prudently placed. Still it was the Saint Laurent shirt with its false modest simplicity that won the day.

Courrèges had out-panted him in 1964, two years before Saint Laurent's first 'smoking', and yet Saint Laurent's more provocatively masculine city pants won him the reputation for putting women into trousers. In 1967 he followed the well-beaten track to the African Exhibition – and out-voodoo-ed the lot with a coat made to look like a witch doctor's straw hut, a safari mini with coq feather topped boots, a see-through dress of wooden beads. History does not relate who wore them.

Spain had always been conceded to be Balenciaga and Castillo country, but in 1968 Saint Laurent found a different Spain – the operatic Spain of Carmen: bullfighters' boleros and high-built matador pants, ponchos, Spanish shawls, combs and flowers behind the ear. It was in this collection that he gave the first hint of the corselet he was to use with such effect in his Carmen collection of 1976 – in a white dress, its deep vee loosely laced together to a high belt. On quite a different tack he had shown himself in sympathy with the King's Road and the *blousons d'ores* of the Left Bank in his near-fatal Beat Collection of 1960. In August 1968 he once more demonstrated his identification with the young – the students' demonstrations, the anti-Vietnam protesters, the growing anger at the plight of the American Indian. He showed his concern in the endless use of sombre black, marchers' headbands, duffle coats, Indian fringes. Once again he seemed unaware of the incongruity of expressing these symbols in terms of Haute Couture – the headbands made of hair plaited by Alexandre, the duffle coats in fur with gold toggles, the fringed buckskins under fox-fur coats. The Bride was a sad little figure in an Oriental tunic and trousers. Fashion was represented by a reiterated use of pants. Of seventy-eight models shown, twenty-eight were pants or jump suits – and this is not counting culottes or Bermuda shorts. As one ecstatic young admirer exclaimed to an unimpressed male artist, 'Why don't you like it? The whole thing's for a man.'

Saint Laurent's last two collections of the decade were uneventful. February 1969 saw the mourning and the headbands dropped for the current minis, maxis and mufflers, to which he added knitted tea-cosy caps, pulled down to the eyebrows. And there were, of course, the inevitable pants. It was a droopy look which, oddly enough, suited the mood of the young, who clung to it well into the Seventies. August saw more minis and maxis – and, blown across the Channel and the Atlantic, the favourites for which addicts of secondhand clothes had been scouring the thrift shops of New York or the Portobello Road stalls of London since 1964: Victorian leg-o'-mutton sleeves, crushed velvet, passementerie, granny dresses.

Thus the decade ended – not quite with a whimper but not with a bang either. Since 1962 Saint Laurent had made many beautiful clothes, dreamed up many ideas that had become part of fashion language. His collections had acquired a 'must' status. He had made many friends, many more fans and was to make even more. The most positive signature in the Paris of the Sixties was that of Courrèges; the Seventies were to be Saint Laurent's. Because he had flirted with so many of the themes which he was to develop in strength later, his previous collections have been spelt out here in such detail – for that reason and the idiosyncratic way he attacks the problem of fashion.

Before, however, the Seventies can be tackled, Saint Laurent took one of the most important steps in his career. In 1966 he opened his first Rive Gauche shop on the Rue de Tournon, and made his debut in ready-to-wear. He was the first – with Cardin close behind – to sense the potential of the young market of the Left Bank, a market to which he was particularly attuned. The enterprise proved a wild success. The cleverly-named Rive Gauche shops proliferated like minks.

In 1979 there were 160 Rive Gauche shops dotted over the globe, as far afield as Kuwait and Hong Kong. In London alone there are five, three for women (the first opened in 1969), two for men (the first opened a year later). In 1976 his ready-to-wear men's clothing was earning just from the United States $50 million dollars; total sales came to $200 million dollars. By that year he had also extended his designing range to 58 ancillary products. The result of this successful expansion will be told, as it should, at the end of the chapter.

Act III found a perhaps over-stretched Saint Laurent still

searching for a major theme. He began 1970 with a triple bill: a couture collection, costumes for a revue at the Casino de Paris starring Zizi Jeanmaire and, of course, his ready-to-wear collection. The couture collection was a reprise of previous collections, repeating his maxi-skirted Carmen dresses and offering a plethora of trousers (twenty-seven out of ninety-one models shown), from Oxford bags, to partner his Twenties Charleston dresses, to crushed velvet pants suits. Perhaps in honour of these and his new venture into clothes for men, he presented his Bride with a Groom, both in white trouser-suits, about which Felicity Green writing in the *Daily Mirror* noted that it was hard to tell the blushing bride from the blooming groom. It was said that Saint Laurent had been too taken up with the revue to give the collection his full attention. In the event Saint Laurent's sequinned jump suits and ostrich feathers were outshone by that old master of spectacle, seventy-seven-year-old Erté. An unkind comment was that as a couturier Saint Laurent was a great costume designer, as a costume designer he was a great couturier.

The Seventies, like the later Sixties, found the couture designers in Italy, New York and London as well as Paris finding inspiration in the great art exhibitions, in old films, in what seemed like rip-offs of the *National Geographic* magazine: ethnic dress from far-away lands – Japan, Hungary, Iran, India, Morocco and, above all, Russia. Saint Laurent was no exception; costume had always fascinated him. Despite his contemporary thinking as expressed in interviews, it was, therefore, perhaps inevitable that in the collection he showed that July he should return to Russia. It is true that it was only briefly, for his travelogue also included China (with chongsams), Japan (with embroideries), British panto with swaggering Puss in Boots capes and plumed beaver hats, and what looked like a random selection from any Chelsea boutique. A curious interjection betrayed his age; having been too young and too far away to have known the hardships of the Occupation, he presented a pastiche of the wartime clothes of defiance – gallant but ugly to later eyes, with their towering turbans, tight, skimpy knee-length skirts, thick pale stockings and clog soles. These amused his devotées who begin clapping in anticipation of their applause cards almost before the model has appeared, shocked others by what seemed a lack of taste. It was said that Saint Laurent thought of them as 'prophetic'. If by 'prophetic' he meant a return to the Thirties and Forties, they did indeed foretell what he was to do. Even more inscrutable was the Bride in a short velvet dress lettered in front 'Love me Forever' and behind 'Or Never'.

His first collection in 1971 was rather unkindly dismissed as a 'tarts' collection. Saint Laurent seemed to have gathered together a bouquet of the tartiest clothes of the late Twenties – and exaggerated them. Pleated hot pants were substituted for short skirts above wedge-heeled shoes, ankle-strapped, worn with seamed stockings, looking strangely naughty in sheer black. He revived the humped and wide-shouldered short fur coats that were to hunch their way into the Thirties and Forties; gave his blazer, now sleeveless and longer, the sharp wide lapels of film gangsters like George Raft. By August of that year the pendulum had swung again – to demure, almost simperingly sweet ruffled and ruched taffeta dresses which he called his 'Proust' dresses. (There was a Proust exhibition at the time.) Actually less Proustian than late Victorian, they were an instant hit and became the popular template for brides and debutantes. As a counterweight he looked to the extended padded shoulders of the mid-Forties, most conspicuously in a belted trench coat which was his most copied model, just as it had been in 1945 ending up three years after on Rita Hayworth – a perfect example of Late Late show inspiration.

His ready-to-wear collection in October of that year, was as crowded as one of his couture collections with celebrities and the jetting editors of American *Vogue* and *Harper's Bazaar* who had flown back especially for the occasion, an excursion that was to become a habit as the interest – and importance – of the French ready-to-wear increased. At that time pants seemed to be forever, (it was not until 1976 that he declared 'pants are finished, there are only jeans today'). Saint Laurent's extra wide trousers worn with sleeveless striped maillots under loose cardigans were enthusiastically received, as were his Little Women gingham checked taffetas. It seemed that Saint Laurent had found a formula: take a period which would touch a sentimental chord in the older women, and seem quite fresh and new to the younger ones. Only a plaintive few were heard to whisper that reminiscence was not fashion.

His July collection of 1972 naturally made a bow to the Chinese exhibition then in Paris, in long slender sheaths (he had already taken over quilting for his ready-to-wear in 1971). China was to become a repetitive theme. The collection was chiefly interesting for his chiffons, which by 1974 had become dreamy wisps of such fragile beauty that British *Vogue* captioned them 'slipstream chiffons'. By 1977 they were to move Diana Vreeland to say, 'Anyone who is thin enough should wear them. They have no business not wearing them.' The 1973 Collection was most conspicuous for his Bride – after all those jokes – a traditional romantic drift of crêpe georgette, her floating train held by a coronet of jasmine. That season he also showed his men's clothes along with his women's for the first time – and jeans (his were pleated into the waist, like the trousers of the Thirties).

Yves Saint Laurent told Polly Devlin in an interview for British *Vogue* in 1974, 'I don't try to make revolutionary clothes every time, I don't try to be sensational but . . . I'm not static in my thinking or emotions or my designing.' He may try not to be a sensation but he succeeds in being one. 1975 was uneventful; 1976 was to be his *annus mirabilis*. That year both his ready-to-wear and his couture collections were each in its own way what could only be called sensational. The first was his Carmen Collection; the other his Rich Peasant Collection. All Paris had, at that mysterious bird-call that only couturiers seem to hear, decided that the time had come to hike up skirts. Each did so in his own way. Saint Laurent chose for his to return to an old love – the Spain of Carmen, an affair he had begun in 1968. His brief flirtations flounced skirts puffing out below teasing corselet bodices, the bobble-edged shawls, the bold colours plus the black velvet neckbands, the flowers in the hair, the black stockings and ankle-laced high-heeled satin slippers, the long cigarette-holders, all added up to what one buyer called provocative. It was all God's gift to photographers. It was also the last recorded appearance of a joke Bride – this time a cancan dancer. One is tempted to paraphrase Marechal Bosquet's remark about the Charge of the Light Brigade: 'It's magnificent, but is it fashion?'

His Couture Collection really shook the fashion world. It had been foreshadowed by his Spring collection, but no one was apparently prepared for its breathtaking luxury and drama. Saint Laurent had never really left Russia since he discovered its fascination in 1966. It appeared to him to be as endless a source of inspiration as it is vast in size, various in native dress and ethnic groups, rich in history. Tsarist Russia – Cossack, Princess, peasant, gypsy – took pride of place, but there was as usual a potpourri of other geographical motifs derived from Morocco, India – probably more. The result was a glut of glamour: the incredible range of colours combined in unexpected contrast; the happy Hippie mixture of textures and patterns; the extravagant use of luxurious fabrics from satin to lamé gauze, from taffeta to mousseline; the full, swelling skirts; vast puffed sleeves, accentuated by cinched-in waists, belted, sashed or swathed; the elaboration of trimmings, with at one end a variety of headgear from babushkas to fur hats, turbans and fezzes, at the other boots. Saint Laurent has been quoted as saying that he had been forced to repress his sense of fantasy and was ready for 'a big burst'. And big burst it was.

Time magazine, with its usual acuteness, noted that by introducing the peasant look first in his ready-to-wear, the less expensive (but not exactly cheap) versions were ready to be on sale at the Rive Gauche shops at the same time as the press was knocking itself out finding superlatives for the expense-no-object couture models.

Not all the compliments were unalloyed; to some the voluminous skirts did not seem to suit contemporary life, others objected to the ethnic emphasis, others to the price ($5,000), but in December when Diana Vreeland opened her exhibition 'The Glory of Russian Costume' at the Metropolitan Museum of Art in New York (a curious coincidence), Eugenia Sheppard in the *New York Post* reported that it was also 'a triumph of a kind for Yves Saint Laurent since at least 60% of the $150-plate-dinner crowd came in his genuine, made-to-order original dresses, top price copies or taffetas inspired by them.' (The price of the dinner has since gone up – but that has not deterred Mrs Vreeland's faithful.)

It is possible to chart a designer's degree of success by the number of pages and covers he rates in fashion periodicals. British *Vogue*, which had been giving Saint Laurent the usual dutiful beautiful spread, in 1976 gave him six pages, in 1977 ten. For his rich peasant collection *Time* magazine gave him two stories on two successive weeks with two pages in colour. As for *W*, from April 1966 when it was the first to give it a front page, has since been covering Saint Laurent so generously and continuously that it seems as if the poor fellow never stops designing and talking.

In 1977 Yves Saint Laurent went through so many moods that it would require a computer memory-bank to recall them all. During the year he went to all lengths – skirt lengths, that is – travelled, from a Laura Ashley Victorian nursery, in naive little girl shifts, ruffled at yoke, neck and hem, to the wilder shores of costume – Tartary, Mongolia, Turkey and Mandarin China. To these he added a souvenir of his 'Proust' period, and then came back to Paris of the Thirties with Schiaparelli-type dinner suits with fitted jackets, high padded and puffed shoulders. He softened the echo of

Schiaparelli's masculine sharpness with soft, ruffled collars. And despite his view of 1976 on pants, they were there in force, in all shapes and lengths. Diana Vreeland, with her wonderful gift of phrase epitomized the collection: 'Yves Saint Laurent,' she said, 'has wandered through history with a sort of butterfly net and he's caught some of the most beautiful attributes of women from all ages.' That year too, besides working on his book which he had begun in 1976, Saint Laurent launched his first fur collection, a new scent Opium, a new cosmetic line and designed the sets and costumes for Jean Cocteau's *The Eagle with Two Heads* (Imperial Russia again), produced by Pierre Bergé. No wonder Saint Laurent lives with a nervous breakdown.

1978 was, by contrast, fairly quiet. Saint Laurent returned to one of his dearly-loved themes – the nautical look as worn on a yacht; tossed in a touch of Morocco (why not, he has a villa there); devised even further variations on pants, from straight and narrow to as full as a clown's; gave brief play to chongsams, knitted, knee-length and high slit, tiny coolie hats (perhaps left over from the Chinese interlude of the season before) or tinier hats forward-tilted. Skirts dropped or climbed, but on top he continued with his Schiaparelli silhouette in shaped jackets with high, humped shoulders.

1979 began with a Highland Fling – the like of which would make any true Scot reel. Saint Laurent seemed slightly confused about which Charles he had based this look upon. In an interview with *W* he mentioned his 'Charles Stuart Restoration look in lace and taffeta'. This would seem to refer to King Charles and the Lely portraits of Nell Gwyn, but the tartans, the kilts, the plaids, the silver buckled shoes are Bonnie Prince Charlie. There's only nearly one hundred years between them but what's a century between friends, and anyway they were both Scots. Saint Laurent plays with the tartan theme, using it in taffeta for a full overskirt; over black velvet knickerbockers ribbon-caught below the knee; for the jabot and ruffled collar and cuffs of a black satin blouse; as a bow on a white frilled shirt with a black velvet bolero; or just as a plaid (scarf to Sassenachs) over a neat short puffed-sleeve suit, deeply cuffed in the tartan. He also married a plaid to a toreador's outfit – rather confusing, that. He tops the suits with real tam-o'-shanters or variations on the berets worn by some of the Scottish regiments. His heart was not entirely in the highlands for he showed some evening dresses in rich Oriental fabrics, and he did not forget a nod or two to his nautical look.

The big bang came in his winter collection when he dropped Scotland for Diaghilev and the Ballets Russes, with brief full skirts in bright colours, some parti-coloured, bellowing out from fitted hip-length tops, worn with tiny Pierrot ruffs and ballet-tied shoes. His coats had fitted bodices above skirts of New Look fullness. The Picasso influence which started with Saint Laurent's acquisition of a Picasso watercolour led him to the Ballets Russes. Or could it have been Mrs Vreeland's 'Diaghilev and the Ballets Russes' exhibition of 1978? Saint Laurent had also acquired another Cubist, Juan Gris. It is rather hard to find the Picasso influence except in a lozenge patterned bodice and a pair of His and Her Harlequin costumes. The important message was fit, and as he introduced it first in 1977, it is fitting, no pun intended, that he should two years later fit in with the general return to fit.

At forty-four, no longer the boy wonder, Saint Laurent preserves a wonderful sense of adventure. What he has is that overworked word 'charisma'. It is not so much what he does but that it is he who does it. Without being too chauvinistic, it is possible to mention that, in London, Gina Fratini had been showing corselets a season before his Carmen collection but without the Spanish flavour. Jean Muir had presented her 'sophisticated peasant' in 1969, and continued to amplify the look until 1971. 1969 was also the year that Bill Gibb perceived the possibilities in the haphazard combinations of Hippy clothing which were later incorporated into Saint Laurent's 'fantasy look', while for pure fantasy Zandra Rhodes was there in 1968, and is there still. Bill Gibb, too, in 1977 had found mind-blowing ideas in his native Scotland. Alas, none of these talented designers has behind them the half-million dollars that Saint Laurent's Russian collection is said to have cost. But money, though lovely stuff, isn't the whole answer. Whatever Saint Laurent does, he does with a dramatic flair, a perfection of production, both in what is shown and how it is shown. Ideas shower like confetti. Some have been dismissed as folklore or theatre. Saint Laurent himself calls them 'fantasy'. It is possible to think of them as escapist, an escape from a dour and often frightening present into a distant period or country or the safety of art or action. But however Saint Laurent's clothes are regarded, no one can disagree with Diana Vreeland's verdict that 'there is a turmoil of imagination there'. And it shows no signs of flagging.

Saint Laurent's success has brought him a luxurious villa in Marrakesh, a magnificent flat filled with rare and beautiful objects. His new House on the Avenue Marceau is considered to be one of the finest in Paris. It's a happy success story – and it couldn't have happened to a nicer guy.

EPILOGUE

Finishing this book as we enter a new decade, I find it hard to say which is in a more confused state – the world or fashion. Just as what used to be dismissed as science fiction has turned out to become scientific fact, clothes like Cardin's tabards, Courrèges 'astronauts' helmets, Ungaro's brass bra and bikini woven of metal and lace, Paco de Rabanne's brief shifts welded of metal discs and chains considered in the Sixties as 'Space Age', now seem, if not conventional, at least to have a certain poetry compared with the Star Wars excesses of designers like Claude Montana. But fashion is resilient: it has survived wars, revolutions, dictatorships, apogees of absurdity and nadirs of mediocrity. It will undoubtedly survive even if it has to tread water till the flood waters recede.

Ernestine Carter
London 1980

BIBLIOGRAPHY

Baillen, Claude, *Chanel Solitaire*, Collins, London, 1973; Quadrangle/New York Times 1974

Ballard, Bettina, *In My Fashion*, Secker and Warburg, London 1960

Balmain, Pierre, *Balmain*, Cassells, London 1964; Doubleday, New York 1965

Barbey d'Aurevilly, J. A., *Of Dandyism and of George Brummell*, trans. Douglas Ainslie, J. M. Dent and Co., London 1897

Barr, Jr, Alfred H., *Masters of Modern Art*, Museum of Modern Art, Simon and Schuster, New York 1954

Beaton, Cecil, *The Glass of Fashion*, Weidenfeld and Nicolson, London 1954; Doubleday, New York 1954

Beerbohm, Max, *The Works of Max Beerbohm*, John Lane, The Bodley Head, Ltd, London 1923

Bender, Marylin, *The Beautiful People*, Coward-McCann, New York 1967

Bertin, Célia, *Paris à la Mode*, Gollancz, London 1956; Harper and Row, New York 1957

Black, J. Anderson and Madge Garland, *A History of Fashion*, Orbis Publishing, London 1975; Morrow, New York 1975

Boutet de Monvel, Roger, *Beau Brummell and His Times*, Eversleigh Nash, London 1908

Bulwer-Lytton, Edward, *Pelham*, Henry Calburn, London 1828

Carter, Ernestine, *The Changing World of Fashion*, Weidenfeld and Nicolson, London 1977; G. P. Putnam's Sons, New York 1977

Twentieth Century Fashion, Eyre Methuen, London 1975
With Tongue in Chic, Michael Joseph, London 1974
Chase, Edna Woolman and Ilka Chase, *Always in Vogue*, Gollancz, London 1954; Doubleday, New York 1954
Charles-Roux, Edmonde, *Chanel*, Jonathan Cape, London 1976
Cole, Hubert, *Beau Brummell*, Hart Davis, MacGibbon, Granada Publishing, London 1977
Connely, Willard, *The Reign of Beau Brummell*, Cassell, London 1940
Croce, Arlene, *After Images*, Adam and Charles Block, London 1978; Alfred A. Knopf, New York 196?
Dior, Christian, *Dior by Dior*, Weidenfeld and Nicolson, London 1957; Ambassador, New York 1957
Franzero, Carlo Maria, *The Life and Times of Beau Brummell*, Alvin Redman, Ltd, London 1958
Freeman, Sarah, *Isabella and Sam – The Story of Mrs Beeton*, Gollancz, London 1977
Gerson, Noel B., *Lillie Langtry*, Robert Hale and Co., London 1972
Gill, Brendan, *Here at the New Yorker*, Michael Joseph, London 1975
Haedrich, Marcel, *Coco Chanel, Her Life, Her Secrets*, Robert Hale and Co., London 1972; Little, Brown and Co., Boston 1972
Hartnell, Norman, *Royal Courts of Fashion*, Cassell's, London 1971; International Publications Service, New York 1971
Hibbert, Christopher, *George IV*, Penguin, Allen Lane, London 1976
Howell, Georgina, ed., *In Vogue*, Allen Lane Penguin Books, London 1975
Jesse, Captain, *The Life of Beau Brummell*, privately printed, London 1844
Lambert, Eleanor, *World of Fashion*, Bowker, New York 1976
LaTour, Anny, *Kings of Fashion*, Weidenfeld and Nicolson, London 1958
Lee, Sarah Tomerlin, ed., *American Fashion*, André Deutsch, London 1976 (Mainbocher by Dale McConathy; McCardell by Sally Kirkland)
Leslie, Doris, *The Desert Queen*, Heineman, London 1972

Levin, Phyllis Lee, *The Wheels of Fashion*, Doubleday, New York 1965
Lynam, Ruth, ed., *Paris Fashion*, Michael Joseph, London 1972
Marcus, Stanley, *Minding the Store*, Elm Tree Books, Hamish Hamilton, London 1975
Melville, Lewis, *Beau Brummell: His Life and Letters*, Hutchinson and Co., London 1924
Mitford, Nancy, *Love in a Cold Climate*, Hamish Hamilton, London 1949; Random House, New York 1949
The Blessing, Hamish Hamilton, London 1956
Moore, Doris Langley, *Fashion Through Fashion Plates* 1771–1971, Ward Lock, London 1971; C. N. Potter, New York 1972
Munro, H. H. (Saki) *Chronicles of Clovis* (The Jesting of Anlington Stringham), Collected Edition, *Short stories of Saki*, John Lane, The Bodley Head Ltd, London 1930
Onassis, Jacqueline, ed., *In the Russian Style*, Viking Penguin, Inc., New York 1976
Palmer, Alan, *The Life and Times of George the Fourth*, Weidenfeld and Nicolson, London 1972
Poiret, Paul, *My First Fifty Years*, Gollancz, London 1931
Quant, Mary, *Quant by Quant*, Cassell, London 1976
Sackville-West, V., *The Edwardians*, The Hogarth Press, London, 1973; Doubleday, New York 1930
Saunders, Edith, *The Age of Worth*, Longmans, Green and Co., London 1954
Schiaparelli, Elsa, *Shocking Life*, Dent, London, 1954; Dutton, New York 1954
Snow, Carmel, with Mary Louise Aswell, *The World of Carmel Snow*, McGraw Hill, New York 1962
Spencer, Charles, *Erte*, Studio Vista, London 1970
Squire, Geoffrey, *Dress, Art and Society*, Studio Vista, London 1974
Summerson, John, *Georgian London*, Pleiades Books, London 1945
Tenenbaum, Samuel, *The Incredible Beau Brummell*, A. S. Barnes, New Jersey 1967

Thurber, James, *The Years with Ross*, Little, Brown and Co., Boston 1957
Vreeland, Diana and Irving Penn, *Inventive Paris Clothes 1909–1939*, Thames and Hudson, London 1977
Waugh, Evelyn, *Scoop*, Chapman and Hall, London 1938
Wharton, Edith, *The Age of Innocence*, Penguin, London 1974; Appleton, New York 1920
White, Palmer, *Paul Poiret*, Studio Vista, London 1973
Woollcott, Alexander, *While Rome Burns*, Arthur Barker Ltd, London 1934

Journals, Periodicals and Catalogues

Catalogue of the Chanel Sale, Christie's, London 1978
Catalogues of the Costume Institute of the Metropolitan Museum of Art:
The 10s, The 20s, The 30s, 1972
The World of Balenciaga, 1973
Romantic and Glamorous Design, 1974
American Women of Style, 1975
Vanity Fair, 1977
Catalogue of Exhibition *Les Ballets Russes de Serge de Diaghilev*, Ville de Strasbourg, 1969
Encyclopaedia Brittannica, 1911
Fashion 1900–1939, Catalogue of Exhibition, Victoria and Albert Museum, 1975
La Belle Epoque (Costume Society, 1967)
High Victorian (Costume Society, 1968)
Harper's Bazaar 1947–1949
Rolling Stone, 11 August 1977 ('A Question of Style' by Lally Weymouth)
The International Herald Tribune
The Listener 12 July, 1979 (Dr Roy Strong)
The New York Times
The Shorter Oxford English Dictionary, London 1933

The So-Called Age of Elegance, Geoffrey Squire, 'Liberty, Equality and Antiquity' (Costume Society, Spring 1970)

The Sunday Times 1955–72

Chanel – from 12 February, 1956

Molyneux – from 20 October, 1963, through July, 1970

Mainbocher – 5 October, 1958, 7 February, 1965, 12 December, 1965, 20 20 October, 1968, 5 September, 1971

Time Magazine

Vogue

Molyneux – 15 August, 1952

Vionnet – 1 October, 1967 (Bernard Nevill)

W, Fairchild Publications

Women's Wear Daily, Fairchild Publications

Vionnet – 21 April, 1969

Index

Adrian, 42
Agha, Dr, 142, 144
Albini, Walter, 114
Alix, *see Grès*
Alphand, Nicole, 123
Anthony, Pegaret, 30
Aragon, Louis, 46
Arden, Elizabeth, 145
Ashley, Laura and Bernard, 209; American venture, 178, 179, 180–1; background, 176, 177–8; shops, 176–7, 178–9
Asquith, Margot, 49
Aswell, Mary Louise, 144, 146
Augustabernard, 77
Austin Reed, 116
Avedon, Richard, 133, 144, 162

Bakst, Léon, 48
Balenciaga, Cristóbal, 27, 63, 92, 94, 95, 97, 100–8, 200; background, 101–2; compared with Dior, 100–1, 103–4; friendship with Vionnet, 36; influence on Courrèges, 131, 132; influence on Saint Laurent, 198, 199; sack dresses, 78, 104; working methods, 103; in World War II, 88–9
Ballard, Bettina, 87, 106; on Carmel Snow, 146; on Diana Vreeland, 163, 165, 167; on Edna Woolman Chase, 142; friendship with Chanel, 150; on Vionnet, 39, 40, 42
Ballets Russes, 48, 56–7, 59–60, 170, 171, 211
Ballien, Claude, 57
Balmain, Pierre, 39, 63, 72, 73, 92, 94, 103
Balsan, Etienne, 55
Barbey d'Aurevilly, 10
Barbier, Georges, 141
Bardot, Brigitte, 124
Barry, Eleanor, 163
Beaton, Sir Cecil, and Balenciaga, 100, 103; designs costumes for *Coco*, 64–5; on Diana Vreeland, 163, 164–5, 166; and Dior, 36, 73, 94–5, 101; on Vionnet, 37, 40; works for *Vogue*, 142
Beaumont, Count Etienne de, 61
Beerbohm, Sir Max, 9–11, 12, 14, 15, 16
Beeton, Samuel, 29
Benda, 141
Benois, Alexandre, 48
Bérard, Christian (Bébé), 87, 92, 93, 94, 141–2, 168
Bergé, Pierre, 194, 196–7, 210
Berman, Eugène, 141
Bernhardt, Sarah, 47
Berthelot, Gaston, 65
Bertin, Célia, 38, 39, 40
bias cut, 36, 37, 42, 125
Blass, Bill, 184
Block, Kenneth Paul, 153
blouses, Vionnet, 41–2
Blume, Mary, 51
Blumenfeld, Erwin, 142
Bobergh, Otto, 27, 31, *see Worth*
Bohan, Marc, 63, 154
Bonwillum, 191

Bouché, René, 141
Bouet-Willaumez, Raoul, 141
Bousquet, Marie-Louise, 93, 94, 143, 196
Boussac, Marcel, 92
Boutet de Monvel, 141
Boyd, Ann, 191
Braniff International Airways, 116, 117
brassière, invention of, 48
Breton, André, 46
Bricard, Madame, 73, 195
bridal wear, Saint Laurent, 201, 203, 205, 206, 207
Brisson, Frederick, 64
Brodovitch, Alexey, 144, 162
Brummell, Beau, 27, 122, 141; 'eschews colour', 8–9; at Eton, 13–14; and George IV, 14–18, 58; innovations, 16, 17; neckcloths, 12, 15–16; in 10th Regiment of Light Dragoons, 14–15; reputation, 8–11, 12
Brunelleschi, 141
Brunhoff, Michel de, 194
bustles, 30, 39
buttons, Schiaparelli, 87, 88
Byron, Lord, 10, 17, 18

Callot Soeurs, 41
Cantor, Eddie, 61
Capel, Boy, 55–6
Capezio (McCardell), 186
Capote, Truman, 162, 165, 171
Cardin, Pierre, 63, 202, 204, 213; background, 124–5; collections, 123–4, 125–6, 127; diversification, 126–7; drapery, 125; L'Espace Cardin, 124; men's wear, 116, 122–3; ready-to-wear, 126; tights, 107
Casa Torres, Marquesa de, 101–2
Cashin, Bonnie, 184; background, 187; colours, 188–9; film costumes, 187; influences, 188; philosophy, 187–8; use of industrial hardware, 88, 188
Castillo, Antonio del, 58, 63
Castle, Vernon and Irene, 167
Cavanagh, John, 72
Cazaubon, Jean, 66
Chambre Syndicale de la Couture Parisienne, 28–9, 51, 123
Chanel, Gabrielle (Coco), 38, 40, 54–66, 70–1, 77, 80, 103, 168; background, 54–6, 58–9; comeback, 61–3; dislike of Schiaparelli, 58, 84; *Garçonne* look, 58, 85–6; Hollywood, 60, 61; influence on Saint Laurent, 202; innovations, 56–8, 60; Mary Quant on, 137; play, *Coco*, 64–5; ready-to-wear, 65–6; *Le Train Bleu* designs, 59–60; trousers, 56, 57, 134–5; use of fabrics, 57, 79, 88; and *Women's Wear Daily*, 150–1, 153–4; working methods, 103
Charles-Roux, Edmonde, 54, 55, 58, 60
Chase, Edna Woolman, 76; edits *Vogue*, 140–2, 145, 146–7; sacks Dorothy Todd, 145; on Schiaparelli, 88–9; on Vionnet, 37
Chelsea, King's Road, 131–2, 133, 196, 203
Chéruit, Madame, 46, 85
Ciano, Edda, 117–18
Claire, Ina, 59, 61
Cocteau, Jean, 58, 59, 60, 87, 88, 124, 145, 210
Colbert, Jean, 28
Cole, Hubert, 8, 13, 14, 15
Colette, 58
collars, Balenciaga, Givenchy, 102; Cardin, 125
colour, Bonnie Cashin, 188; Courrèges, 134; Poiret, 48; Pucci, 116, 117; Schiaparelli 'shocking' pink, 86; other colours, 87
Connely, Willard, 13
Cooper, Gladys, 73
corsets, Dior guêpière, 79; Mainbocher, 78–9; Poiret abolishes, 47–8, 56
Costume Institute, Metropolitan Museum of Art, 36, 89, 100, 164, 170–1, 209
Courrèges, André, 63, 126, 130–7, 202, 204, 213; background, 130, 131, 132;

colours, 134; men's wear, 136–7; ready-to-wear, 136; trousers, 64, 130, 134–5, 199–200
Courrèges, Coqueline, 137
Coward, Noel, 73, 75
Crahay, Jules François, 63, 171
Creed, Henry, 32, 58
crinolines, 16, 22, 26–30
Crosby, John, 133

Dahl-Wolfe, Louise, 144
Daily Mirror, 205
Dali, Salvador, 87, 141, 144
De La Renta, Oscar, 30, 184
denim, 186
Derby, Lord, 71
Dessès, Jean, 92
de Valois, Dame Ninette, 59–60
Devlin, Polly, 152, 207
Devonshire, Georgiana, Duchess of, 9
Diaghilev, Serge, 59, 60, 94, 167, 170, 171, 211
Dior, Christian, 92–7, 196; background, 92; Cardin apprenticed to, 124–5; compared with Balenciaga, 100–1, 103–4; death, 63, 97; influence on Saint Laurent, 194, 198–9; 'New Look', 62, 73, 93, 95, 103, 185; on Vionnet, 36, 42; working methods, 103
Dior, House of, 63, 80, 122, 133, 154, 194–6
Disraeli, Benjamin, 11, 13
Dmitri, Prince of Russia, 55, 59
Dolly, Jenny, 71, 72
D'Orsay, Count, 11
Doucet, Jacques, 37, 41–2, 46–7, 101–2
Drian, 141
Dudel, Yvonne, 66
Dufy, Raoul, 50, 141, 144
Duse, Eleanora, 47

Edward VII, King of England, 25
Elliot, Harrison, 93
Encyclopaedia Britannica, 22
Eric, 77, 142
Erté, 46, 49, 145, 205
Eugénie, Empress, 16, 23, 25–9, 31, 58–9, *see Worth*
Evening Standard, 108, 152

Fairchild, John, and Chanel, 150–1, 153–4; feud with Marc Bohan, 154; gossip column, 150, 151–2, 155; support for Saint Laurent, 154, 157; and *W*, 155–8; and *WWD*, 150, 151–5, 157–8; *see also W Women's Wear Daily (WWD)*
Fath, Jacques, 63, 92
Les Fauves, 48
Fellowes, the Hon. Mrs Reginald, 86–7, 143, 144, 163
Féraud, 63
Fini, Leonor, 86
Fisher, Lillian, 77
Fitch, Clyde, 8
Fleming, Ian, 75
Fontanne, Lynn, 73, 80
Frank, Jean Michel, 87–8
Fratini, Gina, 211
Frissell, Toni, 112–13

Gagelin et Opigez, 22–3, 25–7
Galanos, James, 184
Galitzine, Irène, 130
Garland, Madge, 37, 42, 145
La Gazette du Bon Ton, 50, 141
George IV, King of England, 11, 12, 14–18, 58
Gerber, Madame, 41
Gerson, Noël B., 25
Gibb, Bill, 211–12
Gill, Brendan, 8
Ginsburg, Madeleine, 39, 42
Giorgini, G. B., 114
girdles, 47–8, 117
Givenchy, Hubert de, 63, 97, 104, 200; on Balenciaga, 103; collars, 102; sack dresses, 105; separates in Schiaparelli, 88
Goldwyn, Sam, 60–1

Gramont, Duchesse de, 36
Grandpierre, Victor, 92
Green, Felicity, 63, 205
Greenwood, Charlotte, 61
Grès, 40, 63, 92
Griffe, Jacques, 39
Guardian, 137, *see Polan*
Guibourgé, Philippe, 65–6
Guinness, Gloria, 100, 152, 156
Gwynn, Foxy, 77

Haedrich, Marcel, 54
Hahn, Reynaldo, 8
Halston, 36, 117, 184, 191
Harlow, Jean, 42
Harper's Bazaar, 100, 152, 206–7; Balenciaga and, 104; under Carmel Snow, 140–7, 162, 163; Diana Vreeland works for, 144, 162–4, 169, 185–6; origins of, 140; Pucci and, 113; rivalry with Vogue, 76, 140, 142; and Swinging London, 133
Hart, Moss, 164
Hartnell, Norman, 26, 30, 31
hats, Pucci, 116; Saint Laurent, 210; turbans, Poiret, 48
Haussmann, Baron, 23
Hearst, William Randolph, 140
Heim, Jacques, 58, 88
Henderson, Lady, 180–1
Hepburn, Katharine, 64
Hesketh, Christian, Lady, 167, 171, 172
Hibbert, Christopher, 11–12, 16
hobble skirts, 46, 49, 196
Holzer, Baby Jane, 152
Horst, Baron Horst B., 42, 78, 142
Hoyningen-Huene, Baron George, 76–7, 142
Hugo, Jean, 87

Incorporated Society of London Fashion Designers, 74
International Herald Tribune, 51, *see Blume*
Iribe, Paul, 50, 59, 141
Irwin, Rea, 8–9

jackets, Balenciaga, 104; Chanel, pea jackets, 56, cardigans, blazers etc., 57–8; Saint Laurent, pea jackets, 198, blazers, 201
Janet, Janine, 107
Jeanmaire, Zizi, 198, 205
jeans, 186
Jesse, Captain William, 8, 12, 13, 14, 15
jewellery, Calvin Klein, 191; Chanel, 54, 55, 61; Halston, 191

Kaufman, Beatrice, 144, 162, 164
Kaufman, George, 8, 164
Kirkland, Sally, 70, 79, 186
Klein, Calvin, 184; background, 189–90; jewellery, 191; 'pared down' style, 190–1; and *W*, 190
Klimt, Gustav, 48
Knickerbocker, Suzy, 151

Lagerfeld, Karl, 54–5
Lambert, Eleanor, 189
Landels, Willie, 146
Langtry, Lillie, 25
Lanvin, Madame, 51, 88, 92
Lanvin, House of, 63, 122, 171
Laurens, Henri, 59
Lawrence, Gertrude, 73
Lelong, Lucien, 89, 92, 94, 95
leotards, 186
Lepape, Georges, 49, 50, 51, 141
Lerner, Alan Jay, 64
Levin, Phyllis Lee, 166, 185
lingerie, Mary Quant, 134; Pucci, 117; *see also* corsets
Lister, T. H., 8
Loos, Anita, 84, 143
Lord and Taylor, 113
Louiseboulanger, 77
Lucile, 28, 71, 72
Luling, Suzanne, 93, 197
Lytton, Bulwer, 8

McCardell, Claire, 189, 190; background, 184–5; innovations, 185;

shoes, 186; use of fabrics, 79, 185–6
McConathy, Dale, 78
McFadden, Frances, 143
McManus, Cathy, Marchesa di Montezemolo, 113
McNair, Archie, 131, 137
Mainbocher (Main Rousseau Bocher), 38, 49, 58, 88, 94; background, 70; clientèle, 79, 80; dresses Mrs Simpson, 77–8; edits French *Vogue*, 76–7; innovations, 78–9; salons, 78, 79; theatrical costumes, 79–80
Mansfield, Richard, 8
Marcus, Stanley, 73, 112, 115, 135
Marina, Princess, 70, 74
Marriott, Lady, 95
Martin, Charles, 141
Martin, Mary, 80
Martinez de Hoz, Madame, 36
Marty, A. F., 141
Marx, Groucho, 9
Massaro, 63
Maud et Nano, 93
Maxwell, Elsa, 71, 86
Mazzola, Anthony, 146
Melville, Lewis, 13, 16
men's wear, Cardin, 122–3; Courrèges, 136–7; Dior, 122; Lanvin, 122; Pucci, 116
Mermau, Ethee, 80
Metropolitan Museum of Art, 36, 89, 100, 164, 170–1, 209
Metternich, Princess, 27, 29
Meyer, Baron de, 142
Milland, Ray, 143
Mille, Hervé, 55, 56
Miller, Alice Duer, 8
Miller, Beatrix, 146
Miller, Jonathan, 172
mini skirts, 132–3
Mirabella, Grace, 169
Missoni, 114
Mitford, Nancy, 86, 95, 143
Molyneux, Captain, 58, 94, 103; background, 70–2; clientèle, 72–3; collection of paintings, 74–5; return to fashion, 75–6; salons, 72, 73–4; in Second World War, 74, 88–9; theatrical costumes, 39, 73; and Vionnet, 36, 39
Moore, Doris Langley, 26, 49
Morand, Paul, 56–7
Moreau, Jeanne, 124
Morris, Alice, 185–6
Morris, Bernadine, 180
Muir, Jean, 211
Munkacsi, Martin, 143–4

Napoleon III, Emperor, 23
Nast, Condé, 140–1, 145
neckcloths, 15–16
necklines, Cardin, 125; *see also* collars
Nevill, Bernard, 36, 37, 39, 40, 41
'New Look', 93, 103, 104
New York Herald Tribune, 151, *see Sheppard*
New York Post, 209, *see Sheppard*
New York Times, 180, 186, *see Morris*
New Yorker, 8–9, 133, 165, 170–1, *see Trow*
Newhouse, Samuel I. and Mary, 146
Newsweek, 186
Nijinska, Bronislava, 59
Norell, Norman, 184
North, Lord, 12, 13

Observer, 191, *see Boyd*
Oliver, André, 127
Onassis, Jacqueline, 152, 155

Paley, Mrs William, 152
Palmer, Alan, 16
Paquin, 92, 124–5
Parker, Dorothy, 8, 30, 143
Parnis, Mollie, 150
Patou, 58, 70, 77, 88, 92
Penn, Irving, 36–7, 142, 170
Peretti, Elsa, 191
perfume, Cardin, 126, 127; Chanel, 56, 61; Courrèges, 137; Poiret, 50, 51, 117; Pucci, 117; Schiaparelli, 86
Peyerimhoff, Yvonne de, 197

Picasso, Pablo, 46, 58, 59, 60, 144, 211
Piguet, Robert, 39, 51, 73, 88, 92, 94, 122
Pipart, Gérard, 63
Pitt-Lennox, Lord William, 11
Plunket Greene, Alexander, 131, 132, 137
Poiret, Madame, 47, 49, 51
Poiret, Paul, 27, 46–51, 56–7, 70; hobble skirts, 49; innovations, 47–8, 86; models, 28; pantaloons, 50; perfume, 50, 117; tunics, 49, 50; turbans, 48–50; use of colour, 48
Polan, Brenda, 137
Pope-Hennessy, James, 27
Previn, André, 64
Proust, Marcel, 41, 206, 209
Pucci, Emilio, 135; background, 114–15, 117; beachwear, 112, 113; diversification, 115–16, 117; Indonesian influences, 114; men's wear, 116; political interests, 115; in Second World War, 117–18; shirts, 113; ski wear, 112–13; use of colour, 112, 116–17, 118; use of jersey, 114

Quant, Mary, 130–7, 176; background, 130–1; Bazaar shops, 131; diversification, 136; fabrics, 134; hot pants, 136; mini skirts, 63, 132–3, 135

Rabanne, Paco de, 213
Raikes, Tom, 18
ready-to-wear, American, 184; Cardin, 126, 127; Chanel, 65–6; Courrèges, 136; Saint Laurent, 204, 206–7, 208–9
Redding, Cyrus, 15
Redfern, (Poynter), 32
Reilly, Kate, 41
Réjane, 47
Renée, Mme, 106–7
Reverdy, Pierre, 59
Rhodes, Zandra, 80, 180–1, 211–12
Ricci, Nina, 63, 92
Robinson, David, 170
Robinson, J. Mack, 197, 200
Rochas, 92
Ross, Harold, 8–9
Rothschild, Baroness Pauline de, 100, 101, 103
Rubinstein, Helena, 106, 197–8
Russell, Rosalind, 64

sack dresses, 78, 104–5
Saint Laurent, Yves, 105, 154, 194–212; admiration for Chanel, 63, 202; African Collection, 198, 202–3; background, 194; Ballets Russes Collection, 171, 211; Beat Collection, 133, 196, 203; Carmen Collection, 203, 205, 207, 208; Chinese influences, 205, 207, 210; at Dior, 194–6; Mondrian dresses, 200–1, 202; Moroccan influences, 190, 210; nautical influences, 201, 210; opens his new House, 196–8; padded shoulders, 89; Pop Art Collection, 201, 202; ready-to-wear, 204, 206–7, 208–9; Rich Peasant Collection, 207, 208–9, 211–12; Scottish Collection, 210–11
Salomon, Richard, 200
Samuels, Arthur, 143, 144
Schiaparelli, Elsa, 77, 84–9, 92, 124–5, 201; background, 84–5; Chanel's dislike of 58, 84; closes House, 63; fabrics, 79; men's ties, 122; Saint Laurent echoes, 209–10; trimings, 87–8
Schlumberger, Jean, 87
Sert, Misia, 56–7, 59
Settle, Alison, 41
Sheppard, Eugenia, 151, 209
shoes, Chanel, 55, 63; Claire McCardell, 186
shoulders, padded, 85, 89, 185, 206
Simpson, Mrs, 70, 77–8
Sitwell, Osbert, 48
skirts, bustles, 30, 39; crinoline, 16, 22, 26–30; hobble, 46, 49, 196; midi, 136; mini, 132–3
Snow, Carmel, 185; on Chanel, 59; and Mainbocher, 76; support for

Balenciaga, 100–1, 102, 104; moves to *Harper's Bazaar*, 140–1, 142–7, 162–3, 169; works for *Vogue*, 140, 143
Sorel, Cécile, 42
Spanier, Ginette, 96
Squire, Geoffrey, 48
Stanhope, Lady Hester, 18
Steichen, Edward, 36, 142
Strong, Dr Roy, 11, 122–3
Sullivan, Frank, 185
Sunday Times, (London), 54, 62–3, 65, 75, 100, 104–5, 115, 124, 154, 169
Sutherland, Mrs Graham, 106
Swanson, Gloria, 61
sweaters, Schiaparelli, 84–5

Tchelitchew, 144
Tenenbaum, Samuel, 12
Time, 151, 208–9
The Times, 85, 169, 170
Todd, Dorothy, 145
Toomey, Philippa, 54, 169
Trigère, Pauline, 184
trousers, Chanel, 56, 57, 134–5; Courrèges, 64, 130, 134–5, 199–200; Saint Laurent, 201, 202, 203, 205, 207, 210
Trow, George, 170–1
Tullis, John, 75
turbans, Poiret, 48

Uhry, Ghislaine, 124
Ungaro, 213
Unisex clothes, 126

Véra, Mme, 106–7
Verdura, Duca di, 61
Versace, Gianni, 191
Vertès, 141
Victoire, 197
Vidor, Florence, 59
Vionnet, Madeleine, 30, 36–42, 51, 73, 77; abolishes corsets, 47, 57; background, 41–2; bias cut, 36–8, 125; fagotting, 31, 42
Vogel, Lucien, 50, 141
Vogue, 36, 37, 71, 206–7; on Calvin Klein, 190; Diana Vreeland works for, 140, 144–5, 162, 164–6, 169; rivalry with *Harper's Bazaar*, 76, 140, 142; Saint Laurent in, 209; Schiaparelli in, 86–7; under Edna Woolman Chase, 140–7
Vreeland, Diana, 155; appearance, 164–6; and Baby Jane Holzer, 152; background, 167–9; on Claire McCardell, 185–6; costume exhibitions, 36, 89, 100, 164, 170–1, 209, 211; on Poiret, 51; on Saint Laurent, 207, 210, 212; on Schiaparelli, 85; on Vionnet, 37, 38–9; works for *Harper's Bazaar*, 144, 162–4, 169, 185–6; works for *Vogue*, 140, 144–5, 162, 164–6, 169
Vreeland, T. Reed, 168, 169

W, 169, 210; and Calvin Klein, 190; circulation, 158; contents, 155–7; John Fairchild starts, 150, 155; support for Saint Laurent, 209; *see also* Fairchild, John; *Women's Wear Daily (WWD)*
Warner Brothers, 78–9
Waugh, Alec, 143
Waugh Evelyn, 143
Weldon, Christopher, 29
Wellington, Duke of, 18
Westminster, Duke of, 59
Wetton, Sheila, 74
Weymouth, Lally, 169
Wharton, Edith, 24
White, Nancy, 147
White, Palmer, 47–8,51
White, Sam, 108
Windsor, Duke of, 70
Winterhalter, Franz, 26, 29
Women's Wear Daily (WWD), 58, 137, 163; circulation, 157–8; encourages longer skirts, 136; 'Eye' column, 151–3, 154–5; John Fairchild updates, 150–3; and Saint Laurent, 154, 196, 198; *see also* Fairchild, John; *W*
Woollcott, Alexander, 8, 10

Worth, Charles Frederick, 46, 47; appearance, 32; background, 22–4; bustles, 30; clientèle, 24–5, 27; crinolines, 16, 22, 26–7, 28, 29, 30, 31; dresses Empress Eugénie, 26, 27–8, 29, 59; family, 28–9, 31; Lillie Langtry and, 25; marriage, 25; retirement, 31; works for Gagelin et Opigez, 22–3, 25–7
Worth, House of: Worth, Gaston, 28, 31, 32; Worth, Jacques, 28–9, 36, 51; Worth, Jean Philippe, 30, 31, 32; Worth, Madame, 27, 28
Worth, Irene, 80

York, Duchess of, 13
Yorke, Captain, 18

zippers, Schiaparelli and Bonnie Cashin, 88